Nature's Manuscript

Additional titles from Finn Cara Press:

Birdsong
by Patricia C. Wright

Going to the Dogs
by Richard D. Wright

Tale of the Reed: A Journey of Retreat
by Richard D. Wright

Nature's Manuscript

Patricia C. Wright

Finn Cara Press
Derby Line, Vermont

Finn Cara Press
433 Main Street
Derby Line, Vermont 05830

©2021 Patricia C. Wright. All rights reserved. No part of this publication may be reproduced, stored in a retrieval system, or transmitted by any means, electronic, mechanical, photocopying, recording, or otherwise, without prior written permission.

Cover image by Matt Gibson, courtesy of Shutterstock.com
Cover design by Sandra Lillydahl

Author: Patricia C. Wright (1932-)
Title: Nature's Manuscript
ISBN 978-0-9600949-3-6

Printed and bound in the United States of America

For "all our relations,"
and with thanks to all our teachers, known and unknown

Contents

Foreword 1

Introduction 5

1. Other Ways of Knowing 19
2. Science, Geometry, Pattern and Proportion, Encoding, and More 30
3. The Music of the Spheres 44
4. Light 50
5. Earth 59
6. Earth Energies 64
7. Harmony with the Cosmos 72
8. The Mineral Kingdom and Mountains 77
9. The World of Plants 83
10. The World of Animals 98
11. Air 108
12. The World of Birds 113
13. The World of Insects 119
14. Water 123
15. The World of Fish and Other Water Creatures 130
16. Art 134
17. Children and Nature 144
18. The Garden 149
19. The Green Man 159
20. The Mirror and Transparency 162

Contents

21. The Heart 165
22. Bringing It All Together 171
Notes 173
Suggested Readings 181
Postscript 207

Most people consider as sacred scriptures only certain books or scrolls written by the hand of man, and carefully preserved as holy, to be handed down to posterity as divine revelation. Men have fought and disputed over the authenticity of these books, have refused to accept any other book of similar character, and, clinging thus to the book and losing the sense of it, have formed diverse sects. The Sufi has in all ages respected all such books, and has traced in the Vedanta, Zendavesta, Kabbalah, Bible, Qur'an, and all other sacred scriptures, the same truth which he reads in the incorruptible manuscript of nature, the only Holy Book, the perfect and living model that teaches the inner law of life: all scriptures before nature's manuscript are as little pools of water before the ocean.

To the eye of the seer every leaf of the tree is a page of the holy book that contains divine revelation, and he is inspired every moment of his life by constantly reading and understanding the holy script of nature.

When man writes, he inscribes characters upon rock, leaf, paper, wood or steel; when God writes, the characters He writes are living creatures.

It is when the eye of the soul is opened and the sight is keen that the Sufi can read the divine law in the manuscript of nature.

—Hazrat Inayat Khan, "Sufi Thoughts,"
The Way of Illumination

Foreword

THE SUFIS, as is expressed by Hazrat Inayat Khan, think of nature as the ultimate Book of God, with everything encoded there, waiting to be understood.

The Buddha is said to have given a sermon that consisted of his holding up a single flower. One student understood, and to him the Buddha gave the flower and with it, according to Nancy Wilson Ross, "the tacit honor of transmitting the Great Teaching of 'The Whole,' that single unity or totality which silently expresses itself, and may be fully apprehended in any of its diverse parts."[1]

Mystics from many traditions and indigenous people, both past and present, have also understood nature to be the ultimate teacher.

But today many people still think of nature as a collection of recreation sites, landscapes, Walt Disney–film and cartoon-animal characters, pets, and especially resources—all intended for human pleasure or consumption. As a society most do not think of nature as a sacred teacher, although, fortunately, some individuals still do.

In *Other Ways of Knowing* John Broomfield, himself a historian, wrote that "In the modern West we have made the serious error of equating our way of knowing, which we variously call science and history, with all of knowledge. To put it another way, we have taken a thin slice of reality and mistaken it for the whole. Happily, there are other ways of knowing."[2] His important book reminds readers of many sources of information and wisdom that have been omitted in the current worldview.

Foreword

In *Man and Nature* Seyyed Hossein Nasr wrote that "although science is legitimate in itself, the role and function of science and its application have become illegitimate and even dangerous because of the lack of a higher form of knowledge into which science could be integrated and the destruction of the sacred and spiritual value of nature. To remedy this situation the metaphysical knowledge pertaining to nature must be revived and the sacred quality of nature given back to it once again."[3]

Further on, Nasr wrote, "It must never be forgotten that for non-modern man—whether he be ancient or contemporary—the very stuff of the Universe has a sacred aspect. The cosmos speaks to man and all of its phenomena contain meaning. They are symbols of a higher degree of reality which the cosmic domain at once veils and reveals."[4] And later he added,

> To teach the significance of the tree as the symbol of the multiple states of being, or of the mountain as the symbol of the cosmos, or the sun as the symbol of the intelligible principle of the Universe does not in any way detract from the discoveries of botany, geology or astronomy. But if nature is to be possessed of meaning again . . . this symbolic nature must be presented. . . . The symbolic nature of the tree or the mountain is as closely a part of its being as the bark of the tree or the granite rocks of the mountain. A true symbol is no more man-made than the properties of the bark or the granite.[5]

All these statements are the warp on which this book is woven. My intent is to suggest some of the directions in which we may begin to expand our understanding of nature and of the relationship of the human being with nature, and to offer glimpses into some of the intricacies that a growing awareness of nature reveal, while also suggesting a simplicity at the heart of those intricacies—that it is possible to have a more direct and immediate relationship with nature than we have been taught to imagine. To find that precious connection with nature, known by some of our ancestors and still by some so-called primitive people, or those who have chosen to look to them for wisdom, may well be crucial to the future of human beings on the earth. So although this is a book about some of the wonders of nature, it is also a book about healing our relationship with everything that is—so that we may truly understand and take our appropriate place as part of it all.

Introduction

YOU MAY want to know at the outset the point of view from which I write.

For much of my childhood in Philadelphia my family lived on a street with large sections of Fairmount Park at each end of it, and with only vacant lots on the street behind us, where children played at *Jungle Book* and "rode" imaginary horses. On most Sundays I went on long walks in the woods of Fairmount Park with my father. I took my dog Sandy to the park fields, and with my sister Joan gathered violets in those fields for May Day cornucopias for our mother Ruth, who loved to garden and loved nature but was limited in walking by rheumatoid arthritis. As did many families during World War II, we had a vegetable Victory garden, and my mother always grew flowers; her lovely arrangements were part of the flower shows at the small public school (three grades to a room) that I attended at the end of our street. So I grew up with some awareness of nature and enjoyed being in it, read about it, and looked forward to trips to the shore at Ocean City, New Jersey—as later in life I would love to go to the coast of Maine.

In the early 1950s, by arrangement between the Atlantic Refining Company and the City of Philadelphia, my father, Newell K. (known as Jack) Chamberlin, served on the board and then as executive director of the city's new air pollution control program, so I became aware then of the serious problem of industrial pollution.

Introduction

I studied English literature at Middlebury College and the University of Pennsylvania and received an MA from Middlebury College's Bread Loaf School of English. It was the summers at Bread Loaf and the combination there of a beautiful Vermont natural setting and intellectual companionship that created a desire in my husband Richard and me to move to Vermont at a time when many wanted to go back to the land, although it wasn't until later that we would understand that our choice had a deeper purpose. Although at first we would have liked to continue in graduate school with the goal of college teaching, we later felt it fortunate that life circumstances kept us from that path and sent us on another one, for the new path did not mean the end of learning, but instead opened our minds to new directions of study and changed us in ways beyond anything we once could have imagined.

We moved to rural northern Vermont, where we cultivated gardens and spent as much time as we could outside, but it was not until we had learned how to dowse that the vastness that nature has to teach began to become apparent. Then what had been invisible or unseen began to be revealed, and we learned that one can ask for information that is needed and, once a certain level of awareness is reached, make requests that will be heard.

Most people think of dowsing—if they think of it at all—as exemplified by an old codger crossing a field with a forked stick and waiting for the stick to dip to mark the spot where there is water beneath the earth. That is a primitive version of on-site dowsing. Now many experienced dowsers begin by dowsing on a map, sometimes across the world from the site that is being considered, and both with map and on-site they have learned to simplify their searches and to dowse for precise information about the underground water or whatever else they seek.

Introduction

I first went to a dowsing convention in 1977, curious about what I thought would be water folklore because folklore had been one of my interests in college. I discovered that dowsing is not only folklore or even only about water, but that one can learn not only to dowse from a map or a picture but also for any kind of information, provided that one has both the rational knowledge and the intuitive wit to properly frame precise questions in a binary (yes/no) mode. Having the knowledge from which to frame appropriate questions is very important for accurate dowsing, but beyond that is the need to become centered, with an inner stillness beyond the personality level with all its wishes and fears—a state from which to ask for what one needs to know. Practice in meditation is a great help in achieving that state of inner stillness, and dowsing from such a state is an excellent way to hone intuition and a natural and valid way to obtain many kinds of precise information, as may be judged by the results obtained.

As a form of intuitive knowledge, dowsing is a way of knowing similar to those that, using other names and protocols, are as old as human history. One of the "other ways of knowing," it is a skill that can be learned in our time, step-by-step, by people from all walks of life and age ranges from childhood through old age. Dowsing has great usefulness in enabling us to access information from which to make the kinds of decisions that we all have to make every day. We found it to be an essential life tool, and, although this is not a book about dowsing, I will refer to its usefulness from time to time.

My husband and I were thrilled when dowsing rods and pendulums first moved for us, and we were eager to practice and to learn all that we could. With the progression of learning also came awareness of levels of responsibility that unfold with increasing recognition of the interconnection of all beings and all things and one's consequent responsibility to

Introduction

the Whole—to be manifested in care for the parts—in other words, in the stewardship role. This understanding of stewardship is very different from the idea of dominion over nature that is still rampant in our culture, and also different from the idea of preserving nature for its usefulness to human beings, even unto the seventh generation. Instead, all beings are recognized as kin, but with lives and purposes of their own that may not revolve around or even include us. Respecting the value of those lives has come to be a central aspect of what is now called deep ecology. Although this is not a new idea, it still is not a popular one.

In *Man's Responsibility for Nature* John Passmore wrote that the religion of Christianity, as it developed, encouraged humanity to think of itself as nature's absolute master, an idea originating with the Greeks, notably Aristotle and the Stoics. This view is that nature is to be used as humankind wills, that nature is not sacred, and so relationships with it need not be grounded on moral principles.

An intention of the Protestant Reformation, Rupert Sheldrake wrote in *The Rebirth of Nature*, was the destruction of the idea that the natural world is pervaded by spiritual power, thus preparing the way for the mechanistic revolution in science. Francis Bacon's aim, Sheldrake wrote, was to establish human dominion over the universe, supervised by a scientific priesthood.

Nature became something "to know" in order that its usefulness to human beings could be ascertained. Rene Descartes's view that animals were like machines without feelings came to the fore, and the worldview of mechanistic science has prevailed since that time.

We also have been conditioned to the dominion idea by misconceptions based on that language used in the King James version of the Bible, as well as by social consensus—by what Alfred North Whitehead identified as the powerful

Introduction

but unquestioned assumptions of an epoch. Thus continue the horrible conditions, in both living and dying, for many animals raised for food. Thus laboratory personnel still feel justified in using animals for experiments that they feel may eventually result in help for human beings. Thus the idea of spraying toxic substances on forests or crops, with unknown ramifications for wildlife, for watersheds, for the future, can be seriously considered and too often implemented. And considering nature in a mechanistic way means that people think that they not only have the right to do as they please, but have the illusion that whatever becomes broken as a result of such actions they will be able to fix.

Fortunately, there have always been those who were able to break through the conditioning of their time to espouse worldviews of a sacred universe similar to views held by many indigenous cultures. Over the years mystics of many traditions have realized the unity of creation and the stewardship responsibility of the human being. And in recent years there have been challenges and alternatives to dominion thinking by individuals and groups and books from a variety of spiritual traditions.

Published in 1999, *The Great Work: Our Way into the Future*, written by Thomas Berry, one of the leading spokespersons for the earth in our time, reminds us that our essential human task is to learn how to sustain rather than to exploit our planet home. His message is even more crucial now than when it was written, for it appears to be more and more clear that human beings in far greater numbers will have to make major alterations in their ways of thinking and acting if the human race is to survive. These changes are required not only as a response to climate change, but because of growing realization that all beings in this world are "in this together" and that what happens anywhere affects us all. All beings deserve our respect and care, and we are a very long way

Introduction

from honoring the sacredness of the planet on which we are only temporary guests. Organic and permaculture gardeners and animal and climate change activists have been more aware than many people of this need for change, but there is hope for a growing recognition that many formerly unquestioned assumptions of our time must now be challenged and changed.

When I was in college, as were all others in my biology class, I was asked to cut up a fetal pig. I dreaded the pig lessons that definitely turned my interest away from that field of study. But I never thought that I had an option to refuse to cut up the pig: to not refuse was an unquestioned assumption. So I was pleased many years later to read of the little girl on the West Coast who had refused to cut up a frog in her high school biology class, doing what she could to try to make a difference. The world had changed too, of course, and at this later time a computer program could teach what dissection was meant to show, especially at the level of the need-to-know of the general student taking a required course. But how good it was that Jennifer Graham was able to break through conditioning as she did to make the point that information can be obtained without the needless death of a fellow creature.

Considering our fellow beings primarily for their usefulness to us is a usual and unquestioned assumption of our society, but one that I finally was able to break through myself in 1985. Research on how animals were treated in the commercial food industry, in preparation for my part in a dowsing symposium on planetary consciousness, accomplished that, and life choices had to change to reflect my strong feeling that, once I knew about it, I could no longer willingly be part of that scenario. Also it became clear that vivisection is wrong, and that whatever benefits science may claim result from cruel animal experiments, that is neither the best nor

Introduction

the only way in which we are intended to access information. We had been shown another way to learn, through dowsing, without harm to our fellow creatures.

I was certainly helped along in my learning about the animal kingdom by the presence in our lives of two extraordinary collie dogs, Sean and Brigit, who showed us a great deal about the awareness, intelligence, and kindness of another species. Also our dowser friends included exceptional human beings, who were breaking through a variety of societal assumptions in their own lives and work, especially in regard to the area of consciousness and its relationship to healing. These were not the flaky, fringe individuals that are usually photographed and interviewed by media at gatherings of dowsers, but included Harvard and MIT graduates, scientists, doctors and other medical professionals, and contractors with track records of accomplishments in their business lives as well as in dowsing. In academic life I had never felt the degree of thirst for knowledge that motivated the dowsers we most respected. It was an exceptional climate for learning, and we are very grateful to have been students in the right place at the right time. The dowsers that we most respected were all modest beings, with service to others as their intention. Terry Ross (T. Edward Ross, 2nd), who became our friend and primary dowsing teacher and was one of the world's most skilled and versatile dowsers, always described himself as a "beginner." We are all always beginners, for it is appropriate to remember this: however much we learn or uncover, there is always more to learn. Terry worked in cooperation with and at the request of medical doctors and veterinarians and made many discoveries through dowsing, including information about gene maps that eventually would be affirmed scientifically, although dowsing had provided the answers long before. On one of his early visits to our home I remember Terry coming in and saying, "Take out your pendulums; we're going to dowse about Mars." And so we dowsed then that there was evidence of water on Mars. In 2008 scientists reported that this was so, but again dowsing had given the answer long before.

I was saddened when I read *When God Is Gone Everything Is Holy* by the science writer Chet Raymo, author of many fine books, because in this book he seems to reject the ideas of the soul as apart from the body, of life after death, and of knowledge obtained that is not subject to scientific rigor as defined by repeatable experiments. I agree with much that Chet Raymo has written. Certainly there is magic and mystery in what is around us every day, and the whole point of this book is that nature is the ultimate teacher. But where Raymo draws his line, I wish he did not. Granted that there is much nonsense printed under New Age license, but there is also much that is genuine that comes from other ways of knowing—and often there the "proof" has to be judgment by results.

Raymo seems to lump together almost everything learned outside the discipline of what he feels is replicable scientific method as at least suspect, and he is sometimes not that kind. Yet it is clear by now that experimenters cannot help but influence experiments by their own mindsets, even in the way an experiment is set up. And in experiments using people it is impossible to consider all the variables, that factor alone blurring the results obtained. Jonah Lehrer's article, "The Truth Wears Off" in the December 13, 2010, issue of the *New Yorker*, questions "Is there something wrong with the scientific method?" The article is about how "all sorts of well-established, multiply confirmed findings have started to look increasingly uncertain. It's as if our facts were losing their truth: claims that have been enshrined in textbooks are suddenly unprovable." Lehrer closes his article by saying "The decline effect is troubling because it reminds

Introduction

us how difficult it is to prove anything. We like to pretend that our experiments define the truth for us. But that's often not the case. Just because an idea is true doesn't mean it can be proved. And just because an idea can be proved doesn't mean it's true. When the experiments are done, we still have to choose what to believe." Letters to the *New Yorker* printed in the January 10, 2011, issue brought up still more of the variables that affect test results.

The changing test results Lehrer wrote about at once bring to mind the habits rather than laws of nature that Rupert Sheldrake has suggested.

Chet Raymo is well aware that human understandings about the nature of reality are at best hypotheses and so must be subject to change—that "our knowledge of 'what is' is partial and tentative—a tiny flickering flame in the overwhelming shadows of our ignorance."[1] Later he wrote, "our knowledge has increased dramatically, but so has our awareness of what we do not know. This is perhaps the most important *scientific* discovery of the last century: our ignorance. *Nature loves to hide*. Perhaps her ultimate secrets are hidden forever. Our minds, after all, are finite; the universe may be infinite. We lift the veil, we find another. And another. And another."[2]

One of the most deeply satisfying aspects of our connection with the most accurate and service-minded dowsers that we were privileged to know was to experience the way that they understood and valued both rational/scientific and intuitive knowledge and combined them in their dowsing and in their lives. Although this is not a book about it, I have referred to dowsing quite a bit already because a true dowser uses dowsing all the time, with intuition not just an occasional flash but instead an integral part of the whole process of relating in and to the world. The synthesis that accurate dowsing represents uses rational knowledge to frame precise

Introduction

questions for a dowsed (intuitive) response. The answer is in the question, which means that any bias in the question, any lack, can be reflected in the answer or in the results obtained. To have intuition so developed that it is used with reason in a balanced way is, in my opinion, an ideal toward which the human being would do well to aspire. This book is an attempt to join two kinds of knowing, scientific and other, both valuable, both critical to living fully in this world.

We were most fortunate in friends and generous teachers in those early days of our learning to dowse, and after some years Terry Ross asked my husband to help him to develop a new kind of dowsing school to teach dowsing as related to consciousness. I was pleased to be one of the many field instructors who were invited and who came from across the United States for those two-day schools in which the appropriate field instructor for each student was dowsed. The four years of those schools in Danville, Vermont, from 1984 to 1987 attracted scientists and medical people from a number of countries because of the focus on consciousness, and it was a very special time. Symposia related to consciousness became part of the four-day conventions that Dick and I planned to follow those schools for the final three years. Those who were there during that time continue to call those the golden years of the American Society of Dowsers.

A few years after we began to dowse we also became students of Pir Vilayat Inayat Khan of the Sufi Order in the West (now known as the Inayati Order or Inayatiyya), an organization based on the teachings of Hazrat Inayat Khan, Pir Vilayat's father. Pir Vilayat was interested in dowsing and invited us to speak about it at a retreat he led on intuition. He also wrote to my husband that he planned to use the instructions in *The Divining Mind*, the book that Terry and Dick wrote based on their dowsing school, to find water that so far had not been found where he went in the Pyrenees to

Introduction

have quiet to write his books and articles. Pir Vilayat's form of teaching was very comfortable for us, since it included truth wherever it is found and honored the essence shared, although with different interpretations, by many world traditions. Pir Vilayat was also intensely interested in modern physics and biology, and we first heard of David Bohm and Rupert Sheldrake from him. Under Pir Vilayat's aegis conferences connecting leaders from many different religious traditions, healing conferences including allopathic and other medical and native and spiritual healers, and the formation of the ongoing Omega Institute took place. Within the framework of his teachings we felt that we had come *home*, where all that we cared about and believed was welcomed in a climate of freedom, and where we were introduced to a whole body of Sufi literature and information of which we had no previous awareness. Many doors opened. We began to investigate new material and to read eagerly and widely. Eventually, with permission, we offered classes to others and continued to do that while still, of course, learning ourselves. These classes, with a universal focus that reaches to the heart of authentic traditions, have been intended to enhance and deepen individuals' understandings of their own religious and spiritual choices, identifying common threads that connect while honoring diversity in those paths. Our perspective has been similar to that of Chet Raymo's view of "any religion worthy of humankind's future."

Sufis are described by some as the mystics of Islam, and it is true that, as in the time of Ibn 'Arabi and Rumi (in the twelfth and thirteenth centuries AD), Sufis were sometimes honored in Islam, at least within those communities that showed openness to other religions. Ibn 'Arabi could say that his heart had "become capable of every form" and list differing world scriptures and places of worship as forms with which he was comfortable in the religion of Love. Rumi could say

Introduction

(in the version of Coleman Barks) that all religions are "one song," with only illusory differences, just as sunlight looks different as it falls on different walls but is "still one light."

This Sufi perspective is not welcomed by extremist Muslims of our time (who are only a small part of the Muslim world, appearing not really to understand the true nature of Islam)—nor would this perspective be welcomed by most fundamentalists of any faith—and reasons why will become apparent if you study Sufi literature. There is in this tradition an openness to diversity and a sense of interconnectedness with everything that is that is not part of any kind of narrow fundamentalist thinking in any religion but is, however, reflected in the mystic traditions of many faiths. The term *sufi* has many possible derivations: some think it refers to purity or wisdom, others that it refers to the wool cloaks worn by early Sufis in emulation of followers of Jesus.

I would like to make it clear that our understanding of the impulse that we call Sufi is that it has existed from time immemorial, long before its cultural expression in Islam. The lineage may be traced back to Seth, son of Adam, who in parallel traditional lore was known as Agathadaemon and was the teacher of Hermes Trismegistus, Egyptian sage and founder of Hermeticism, as is mentioned by Pir Zia Inayat Khan, Pir Vilayat's son, in his introduction to *Green Hermeticism: Alchemy and Ecology*. The Sufi impulse is still developing and continues to take its expression from the people, the place, the time, and with the flavor of whatever society it enters.

My husband, who died in 2012, reviewed books, and a number of books and internet postings coming to his attention made the point that the path they refer to as the Sufi path is the best hope for reconciling in the world today differences that are becoming increasingly inflammatory, particularly with the rise of extremist fundamentalist sects with-

Introduction

in all the Abrahamic religions. This understanding of "Sufi," released from the boundaries of cultural expression through Islam, contains all other authentic teachings and allows one to follow a personal path while still being part of a wider community of seekers. Authors of supportive statements in those publications that Dick read were from many different traditions. One noted that he could continue in his Anglican tradition and yet be part of this universal faith. The Israeli ambassador to India was quoted as calling Sufism "the only tool which could retain peace and harmony in the world" and saying that the Sufi is found in both Judaism and Islam. Another author likened Sufi practice to the teaching of karma yoga in the Hindu tradition. Sufism in this understanding is a tradition that, while honoring the diversity of different paths, encourages awareness of that which connects them all. Sunlight shining through shards of differently colored glass appears different but is "still one light." Everything is part of the One, so there is divinity in everything.

My husband and I have not called ourselves Sufis. That designation to us has implied a degree of awareness and dedication that many may aspire to but that few are able fully to attain, so we have honored those beings who were and are genuine Sufis with that term and consider ourselves instead to be among students of this path—and very grateful for what we have learned and been able to incorporate into our lives. We preferred anyway not to use labels, for labels too often become boxes that constrict. But we have tried to be humble followers of the Sufi way, understood in its broadest sense as a universal way that is suggested through and is part of many spiritual traditions.

This book emerges from a series of talks and classes that I gave for our nonprofit Center for Awakening on the relationship of human beings to nature, as well as additional classes on various aspects of nature offered as community outreach

Introduction

over the years. The intent, with a sort of "scatter technique," is to help to lead readers beyond surface appreciation toward greater awareness of some of the many intricacies and subtle lessons in "nature's manuscript." I have included information gleaned from many sources, including some of which you previously may have been unaware; at least that is my hope—to help to make this material more widely known. This may be true of the more esoteric sources on aspects of nature and also of the Sufi sources, for although Coleman Barks's versions of Rumi have been called the best-selling poetry in the United States, most people are unaware of Sufi literature, as we also were unaware of it for many years.

Time now to "get on with it." This is not intended to be a comprehensive covering of the subject matter, but rather an attempt to offer some glimpses into nature's manuscript that may encourage you to investigate further. There are so many books now in the world—nobody can read them all. I have found the sources mentioned to be of value and, while I am still on this earth, would like to leave some record of my search in case it could be of use to someone else. Included too are some of my own special interests. In offering this overview and guide toward further reading, I trust that you will remember that I am a beginner and that there is always more to learn.

I very much appreciate the help of Cannon Labrie and Sandra Lillydahl in preparing this book for publication, and of Al Marin for his computer assistance.

1
OTHER WAYS OF KNOWING

WE ARE blessed in our time to be aware of many knowledgeable, wise, and caring people who have written about nature. Henry David Thoreau, John Muir, Rachel Carson, Paul Shepard, Chet Raymo, Peter Matthiessen, Barry Lopez, Annie Dillard, Joanna Macy, Thomas Berry, Stephen Harrod Buhner, and Mary Oliver come immediately to my mind as the beginning of a long list to which many other names of well-known authors could be added.

But there are other slants and contributions to a broad understanding of nature. Some of these come through scientific, historical, and literary sources, but others come through more esoteric ones. John Broomfield's *Other Ways of Knowing* is an excellent overview of his title, although I am sorry that he did not include dowsing. As I mentioned in the foreword, Broomfield says that we in the modern West "have taken a thin slice of reality" (science and history) "and mistaken it for the whole." Unfortunately, what Broomfield calls a "thin slice of reality" is all that most people are taught or know. Fortunately, there are other ways to access information.

Dowsing

Dowsing is the other way of knowing that I know the best, and from other dowsers we learned a great deal, even beyond that craft. Christopher Bird, as was Dick, was both a trustee and an editor of the *American Dowser*, and we read Chris' book *The Divining Hand* and also those coauthored with Peter Tompkins—*The Secret Life of Plants* and *Secrets of the Soil*. A Harvard graduate, Chris knew a number of languages, had many international contacts, and was always aware of and ready to share the latest information on dowsing, psychic discoveries, and medical progress throughout the world. Frances Farrelly, also an American Society of Dowsers (ASD) trustee, had been involved in esoteric medical studies, had worked with Stanford Research Institute on mind-reach studies, was a trained medical technician with her own laboratory and, when we knew her, taught doctors and other medical people how to dowse. Another Harvard graduate, Terry Ross, had dowsed in many places abroad and had a network of contacts to keep him apprised of dowsing activities and discoveries worldwide. He became a mentor to Sig Lonegren as Sig studied earth energies, and that kind of information also came our way. And we were pleased to be able to meet and to spend some time with Reshad Feild, whose books, especially *Here to Heal*, contain many important insights and instructions about relating to the land.

We learned to dowse underground streams of water and to find out their quality, rate of flow, and depth—both on-site and on maps. We learned how to find energy leys and chi lines and so to become aware of at least part of the esoteric anatomy of the earth. We dowsed for information from which to make decisions about food and matters related to health and healing. And we learned, when we had received the permissions, how to make requests that would be honored in nature through the cooperation of the various kingdoms. We dowsed for auras of people and of plants and animals and learned of the subtle anatomy that all living beings have. We began to "talk" to other beings, on this earth plane and beyond, intuiting and asking questions in a binary mode and dowsing the answers.

Dowsing became for us an essential way to access information from which to make decisions—and an entrance to learning how better to communicate with other beings.

Kinesiology (Body Knowing)

Many people know a little about kinesiology, the muscle testing used by some holistic practitioners to determine whether a food or medicine is good for a patient. I first read of muscle testing in *Your Body Doesn't Lie* by John Diamond, MD. To find that your body can know something of which your rational mind is unaware is surprising, because we haven't been brought up to recognize this possibility. Beginners learning to dowse are sometimes put off when they notice slight muscle movements accompanying a dowsing response, but of course this is so: your body is the medium through which to receive the message from pendulum or L-rod or Y-rod. Kinesiology is a useful other way of knowing and can be a helpful corroboration for some kinds of dowsing.

Another form of body knowing is used by some for dowsing. Machaelle Small Wright of Perelandra teaches the making of a circuit with the thumb and middle finger of the non-dominant hand, then using the thumb and adjacent finger of the dominant hand to press up against this circuit as or after the question (in binary mode) is being asked. If the circuit holds, the answer is yes; if it breaks, the answer is no.

Your body "knows," and kinesiology is one way to access that knowing. A practitioner tests muscle strength of the patient with the patient both holding the food or medicine or with it on the body and also tests without the substance there. This may even be done in a surrogate situation, with the true patient not present. Muscle strength indicates a positive response, weakness a negative one. There are subtleties and discrepancies to be learned about, but that is the general rule. Kinesiology is a very useful technique, and if people are aware of it they generally easily can move on to accepting the idea of a dowsing response.

Intuition

Voices of the First Day by Robert Lawlor, the novel *Mutant Message Down Under* by Marlo Morgan, and the Napoleon Bonaparte mystery series by Arthur Upfield include information about Australian Aborigines and how they relate to nature, including their way of going walkabout without maps or food supplies. They follow "songlines" in the landscape, the stories of the ancestors in the creation of the landscape, and know where to go in what most would perceive as trackless desert, trusting the universe to supply them with what food they need. We are used to the idea of tracking animal footprints, but to be able to track someone over stony ground months after he has passed that way is a skill that must rely more on intuition than on terrestrial signs.

Broomfield wrote about Polynesian navigators who had knowledge of star paths, the habits of migratory birds, and the patterns of light and motion of waves and currents. These navigators had the power to rise in spirit above the masthead to see beyond the horizon, and if further help was needed, guardian spirits could be summoned in animal or fish form to direct them. In *Sacred Geometry* Nigel Pennick shows a geometric shape used to help young Polynesian boys learn how to navigate far from land by recognizing subtle signs, in this case the way patterns of the waves react to the presence of islands.

In our culture we have not been taught to notice or to honor signs, to be aware of earth currents, to go "out of body" for information, or to ask for help from other kingdoms when help is needed, although we can learn to do all these things.

And in our culture we have also forgotten, and most of us have not been retaught, to value our natural intuition or to train it. More attention is being paid to this recently with workshops and books related to developing this skill. Medical intuitives like Carolyn Myss are now sought out, but of course this is not a new possibility. Edgar Cayce's books were once very popular. Fran Farrelly is "Kay" in *Breakthrough to Creativity* by Shafica Karagulla, MD, a book that describes many medical intuitives. Fran's way was to feel in that part of her own body what was being felt by the patient. One doctor described in Doctor Karagulla's book could see and diagnose from the force fields around his patients' bodies, although he was always careful to check these diagnoses with normal examination and laboratory procedures. These forms of higher sense perception are not as rare as you might think, and they can be developed. In fact, psychiatrist Arthur Deikman wrote that "Sufis assert that the awakening of man's latent perceptual capacity (intuition) is not only crucial for his happiness but is the principal goal of his current phase of existence—it is man's evolutionary task."[1]

Frances E. Vaughan's *Awakening Intuition* is a basic book on intuition. She says that "intuition is true by definition," and that if what has seemed to be an intuitive insight turns out to be wrong, then it is not intuition but is instead self-deception or wishful thinking. Her book contains exercises to help to develop true intuitive insights.

Intuition can be accessed in a number of different ways, but learning to dowse is an excellent training because one learns to ask for a specific target or piece of information and to access only that. For example, if one asks for a vein of flowing water and then walks across an area with L-rods, such a vein is all that should be found—not a water pipe nor a sewer line nor groundwater, but only a vein of flowing water. The search can be more clearly defined: please show me only any water vein less than twenty-five feet deep, with a quality of eight or better on a ten-point scale (ten being the best possible water), and with a year-round flow of at least five gallons per minute. Such a vein, if there is one, then should be all that the dowsing rods indicate. Dowsing requires development of one-pointedness, a kind of concentration that allows for a clear answer rather than a vague feeling.

In the annual dowsing schools from 1984 to 1987 in Danville, Vermont, this kind of dowsing was taught on-site by having students first dowse on house lots in the village where the owners had given permission for this exercise. These properties had all been previously dowsed and mapped by Terry and Ginny Ross and Dick and me, and we had recorded the water veins and water and sewer pipes, including those no longer in use. Then, as a double-check, our maps had been verified by the man who had put in most of those water and sewer lines and had records showing their locations. On the second day of the school students were taken by bus to properties where wells had already been drilled and on which we had all the data of water depth, quality, and rate of flow. The students thus had verified results against which to measure their own beginning dowsing efforts.

Learning to dowse can best be done with a great deal of verification in its early stages—to make students aware of and then help them to avoid self-deception and wishful thinking. Suggestions about how to do this are given in *The Divining Heart*. It is very important to build up a track record of accuracy so that when one is ready for intangible dowsing for information, one can have confidence in the results obtained.

Also, as mentioned before, in information dowsing the degree of precision of the question determines the precision of the answer obtained. Learned step-by-step and with many opportunities for verification, learning to dowse is the best way I know of in our culture to hone intuition.

Other Ways of Being

In *The Death of Religion and the Rebirth of Spirit* Joseph Chilton Pearce points out that, although our society assumes "that technology and science are the highpoints of evolution," evolution has "nothing to do with the objective, physical devices brains create for altering their environment." He says that "Our move beyond violence, war, and hatred would be a high-water mark of human evolution." In the meantime we "are changing ourselves and destroying nature by the virtual reality we create." Our brains are changing so that we are not aware of other ways of being. He refers to Dutch psychologist Robert Wolff, who spent several years associated with the Senoi people of the Malaysian rain forest and was eventually initiated into their cosmology and structures of knowledge. "He became aware of the profound setback in evolutionary development that Western humans and our Eastern counterparts have undergone. His conclusion and lament: we have no idea what we have lost."[2]

Pearce says that a society with a "brain system involved in states of consciousness might never be comprehended or even perceived by an object-oriented brain-mind capable only of re-creating objectified things and altering nature and, at the same time, knowing nothing of subjective internal states or experience. . . . Only a brain-mind that had likewise developed could comprehend and resonate with such beings."[3]

Even as other creatures seem to inhabit universes in many ways unique to each species, so human beings with different histories of brain development may have entirely different ways of relating within their worlds. That we do not realize this and so do not try to learn something about the lessons contained in this fact is another of the limitations with which our societal views blinder us.

Shamanism

Lately there is increasing interest in shamanism. Traditionally, shamans were born to the role or chosen, often after protracted near-death experiences. Their task is to become

Other Ways of Knowing

ambassadors between their people and the worlds above and below. Psychically journeying through arduous ordeals, and often with the help of animal guides and helpers, they bring back answers or healing. Today there are many books on shamanism: Michael Harner's *The Way of the Shaman* is a good introduction. Harner, Sandra Ingerman, and other students from the Foundation for Shamanic Studies have taught workshops and written books to help ordinary people develop shamanic skills for solving everyday life problems. Many are now drawn to this path.

In *Dreamtime, Concerning the Boundary between Wilderness and Civilization*, Hans Peter Duerr wrote of an anthropologist who could communicate with a "magic coyote" because something "stopped" in him—that is, his ordinary perception of the world. Duerr mentions patronizing analyses of shamanic thinking, such as "Don't the Indians know that the shaman is only *pretending* to suck the illness out of his patient, that all he has in his mouth is an ordinary pebble that he spits out after sucking?" Duerr responds,

> I should like to propose that we are the ones who lack *their* insight. For just as the coyote turns into a magic being for the person who has eyes to *see*, or rather, *shows* its magic essence, a "mere" stone changes into an evil spirit for the Guiana Indians, and the ancestor appears to the masked dancers.
>
> It is not a "demythologizing," as proposed by critics . . . when it is revealed to the initiates that the humans *themselves* are the ones to perform the dance. Instead, the initiates learn that their persons extend into the depth, that they themselves are the ancestors, whom they used to think of as beings having an existence apart.[4]

Animal Communication

An outgrowth of shamanic techniques is the field of animal communication. We can learn to sense (some by sight, others by sound or by feeling) what an animal thinks and to engage in dialogue with it. This can happen with both physically alive animals and with those that have gone on to the spirit world.

The question arises of how to evaluate what we receive: most important, is it true? Judgment by results is one criterion.

In an animal communication workshop taught by Julie Soquet here in Vermont, several blocks from where our three sheltie dogs remained at home, I received a surprising message explaining a health issue of his from our sheltie Liam, something that would otherwise never have occurred to me. Verification of the message came from the teacher, but even more importantly from the way Liam greeted me when I came home, so excited and happy that I had received his message and could respond to it.

And dogs do know much more than most people realize, as Rupert Sheldrake shows in *Dogs That Know When Their Owners Are Coming Home*. Ours certainly did know that. One graphic example was when my husband was returning from a gathering many hours away. I knew about when he was starting home and noted a time several hours later when the dogs suddenly became very agitated. Later I learned that was the precise time when he drove off the thruway about two hours away from home in order to buy some special cheeses and olives from a favorite store, the Hanover Co-op. The dogs, who had missed him a lot, were temporarily distressed because he was no longer on the direct path home.

Many dogs are also much more aware than we are of what to us is most often invisible. Many people note their pets gazing at what seems to them to be empty space. When finally Liam understood that I was interested in what he saw, he began to come to tell me when an invisible-to-me being appeared. I would then have to dowse who it was, and when I had accomplished this, Liam would go and lie down, satisfied. This is similar to the way our collie Brigit let me know of the presence of invisible-to-me beings, as I described in *The Divining Heart*. Brigit would come and sit in front of me, staring, until she had my attention and I had picked up my pendulum.

Dreams

Dreams are another way of knowing and one that has been used over a very long time. *Conscious Dreaming* by Robert Moss is a good introduction. I particularly value his *Dreamgates* for its accounts of dreaming in different spiritual traditions. In many traditions dreams are considered an important source of spiritual direction, and students are taught before sleep to pose questions that they hope will be answered through their dreams.

Personal insights may be gained from recording and thinking about our dreams. There are books assigning meanings to various dream symbols, but a better way seems to me to be one that a number of dream workers have taught. Have the dreamer tell the dream to the group and then go around the circle with each person saying, if that dream had been his or hers, what it might have meant. This is done without eye contact with or comment from the dreamer, who is free then to accept or reject in silence what has been suggested.

Many scientists have reported that the impetus for a discovery was an image from one of their dreams. Reverie is a form of daydream in which the mind seems to float free, and I have found in reverie a valuable pool from which creative ideas arise. It is similar to using "soft vision" in looking, allowing to come to attention sights or ideas that are there, but that with your usual ways of looking or thinking you would be likely to miss.

Meditation

Other ways of knowing are through meditation and also through getting into the consciousness of other beings, as is

Meditation

taught in some spiritual traditions. The latter is what Reshad Feild and his students call "reversing space." When you see as an animal or a tree or an aspect of weather, you "know" differently than you would know as what you consider to be "yourself." Many seers and shamans have done this, and I think of the early Irish poet, the Milesian Amergin, with his statements: "I am a stag . . . a flood . . . a wind . . . a hawk . . . a salmon." The Robert Graves version incorporates a poem by Taliesin, the Welsh bard, and there are similar statements in other traditions; for example, there is something similar in The *Egyptian Book of the Dead*. These statements may be understood to refer to the Divine manifesting in different forms, to shamanic awareness, to the reversing of space, or to the kind of evolving progression of the soul from mineral to plant to animal to human and beyond of Rumi's poem, in the Coleman Barks version called "An Evolving Course."

These are some of the other ways of knowing and of being that have proven valid with judgment by results over a long period of time. I hope that you will include some of them in your learning because of the many ways that they can add to and enrich knowledge gathered in more familiar ways.

In "Two Kinds of Intelligence," Rumi, in this Coleman Barks version, differentiates between the collecting of information and heart or intuitive intelligence. The latter he describes as

> A spring overflowing its springbox. A freshness
> in the center of the chest. . . .
> This second knowing is a fountainhead
> from within you, moving out.[5]

Both kinds of intelligence are needed, and both need to be valued.

2
Science, Geometry, Pattern and Proportion, Encoding, and More

WE HAVE been taught that the world manifests through pattern and proportion, but few have even a beginning understanding of what this may mean. This chapter is intended to suggest ways to start to think about this statement.

Physicist David Bohm suggests that a way to think of what we experience of our world and universe is expressed in hologram theory. With a coherent light shining through even a tiny part cut from a negative of a holographic picture, the whole may be viewed as reconstituted, although with diminished clarity. Theoretically at least, as one possible ramification of what William Blake suggested, we can "see a world in a grain of sand / And a heaven in a wild flower." The pattern of the whole is shown in the part.

In a similar way many spiritual traditions suggest that what we perceive here in this world is a paler reflection of what exists elsewhere, although there is considerable diversity in the understanding of what and where that "elsewhere" means. But the corollary of that thought is that we can learn about that elsewhere from what is here.

The hologram theory suggests that the world we know is really a virtual reality. Massimo Citro, MD, says in *The Basic Code of the Universe: The Science of the Invisible in Physics, Medicine, and Spirituality* that

> Humans generally believe that everything that happens is grasped by the senses, but it is not so. Our neurons can process only a fraction of the signals we receive from the environment,

as if there is a screen up between us and nature that only allows through some light, sound, and tactile frequencies, which are then translated into *mental images*. . . .

To the incompleteness of our senses we need to add the subjectivity of our processing. . . . We are "blind to the world"; we are not looking outside, but rather *inside* our own heads. We are reading from the brain, watching a film that runs on our cortex. We are prisoners of an inner world, of a machine that produces a virtual reality. So it ends that the senses—our only means of contact with the external world—keep us separated from it through representations that are not real. . . .

The fact remains that we perceive only a negligible portion of the vibrating ocean in which we are immersed.[1]

Pearce wrote that we "are changing ourselves and destroying nature by the virtual reality we create." This statement, as I understand it, refers to the folly of human focus on technological development that is not integrated into a wider and spiritual worldview, as Nasr also warned, and also to the way in which our heavy use of certain technologies themselves are changing our brains. When Citro said "We are prisoners of an inward world, of a machine that produces a virtual reality," he was writing about the limitations of perception through the senses as we have been taught to perceive through them. Part of spiritual unfoldment is learning to develop our senses beyond those perceived limitations.

We can be cognizant of these issues, but we still have to function in this world as it and we ourselves are now perceived by us, so much of this book will be about trying to do that with as much grace as possible, while always being aware of our partial awareness and of the much greater Whole of which we are a part. And later in this chapter there will be more about the explicate order (the world as we experience it) and the implicate order (the more real reality, the world of possibility not yet manifested).

As mentioned in the foreword, the Buddha is said to have given a sermon that consisted of his holding up a single flower. One understanding of the Buddha's action is that the flower expresses the Unity of the Whole, for the Whole may be at least partially perceived, as with the hologram, through any of its diverse parts.

György Doczi began *The Power of Limits* with this flower sermon, writing,

> If we look closely at a flower, and likewise at other natural and man-made creations, we find a unity and an order common to all of them. This order can be seen in certain proportions which appear again and again, and also in the similarly dynamic way all things grow or are made—by a union of complementary opposites.
>
> The discipline inherent in the proportions and patterns of natural phenomena, and manifest in the most ageless and harmonious works of man, are evidence of the relatedness of all things. . . . Perhaps the message of the Flower Sermon has to do with how the living patterns of the flower mirror truths relevant to all forms of life.[2]

Dozci wrote that patterns are defined by their limits and "exemplify an epigram attributed to Pythagoras, that *limit gives form to the limitless*. This is the power of limits."[3]

We realize that we can only begin to understand the limitless through the world of forms. Matter "manifests through pattern and proportion," so it would seem, recalling the "as above, so below" dictum of alchemist Hermes Trismegistus, that form must communicate at least something about what we think of as beyond form.

A word Doczi coined, *dinergy*, means the universal pattern creating process across or through opposite energy—in other words, growth through what is complementary, through purposeful duality.

Science, Geometry, Pattern and Proportion, Encoding, and More

> Take for instance a daisy. The pattern at its center ... the florets that make up this pattern ... grow at the meeting points of two sets of spirals, which move in opposite directions, one clockwise, the other counterclockwise. ... These spirals are logarithmic and also equiangular, since the angle they describe with the radii remains always the same.[4]

As new leaves grow on plants, the leaves climb in a spiral around the stem, as described by Nader Ardalan and Laleh Bakhtiar in *The Sense of Unity: The Sufi Tradition in Persian Architecture*. From leaf to leaf is a fraction of a complete rotation around the stem, this fraction always relating to the Fibonacci series.[5]

In the Fibonacci series numbers in the series are the sum of the two previous ones, and numbers in the series divided by the following one approximate 0.618, and divided by the previous one approximate 1.618. These are the proportional rates between the smaller and larger parts of what is known as the golden mean or golden section.

In *Sacred Geometry* Robert Lawlor wrote, "The Golden Mean spiral ... is found in nature in the beautiful conch shell *Nautilus pompilius* which the dancing Shiva of the Hindu myth holds in one of his hands as one of the instruments through which he initiates creation."[6]

The spiral has also become a symbol of the soul moving toward eternal life or of moving toward the center. Jill Purce's *The Mystic Spiral: Journey of the Soul* explores this ubiquitous symbol in depth. Lawlor also wrote,

> Both our organs of perception and the phenomenal world we perceive seem to be best understood as systems of pure pattern, or as geometric structures of form and proportion. Therefore, when many ancient cultures chose to examine reality through the metaphors of geometry and music (music being the study of the proportional laws of sound frequency),

they were already very close to the position of our most contemporary science....

The point of view of modern force-field theory and wave mechanics corresponds to the ancient geometric-harmonic vision of universal order as being an interwoven configuration of wave patterns.[7]

Lawlor goes on to say that the role of geometry and proportion become even more evident in biology when we understand that all the time "every atom of every molecule of both living and inorganic substance is being changed and replaced." Within five to seven years everyone "will have a completely new body, down to the very last atom.... The carrier of continuity is not only the molecular composition of the DNA, but also its helix form. This form is responsible for the replicating power of the DNA.... The architecture of bodily existence is determined by an invisible, immaterial world of pure form and geometry."[8]

Rupert Sheldrake's description of morphic and morphogenetic fields comes immediately to mind, fields that seem to relate to Bohm's understanding of the implicate order and that replicate ideas and forms. We will come back to this later.

Lawlor went on to write of plants that can carry on photosynthesis because parts of the chlorophyll molecule are arranged in a twelve-fold symmetrical pattern "rather like that of a daisy." In myth the number twelve often occurs as the universal mother of life, and he found this precise, even down to the molecular level, reflecting the innate geometry of life. The sense organs function in response to geometrical or proportional differences: when we smell a rose, we are responding to the geometry of its molecular construction rather than to chemical substances. "Our different perceptual faculties, such as sight, hearing, touch and smell are a result then of various proportioned reductions of one vast spectrum of vibratory frequencies... a sort of geometry of perception."[9]

Science, Geometry, Pattern and Proportion, Encoding, and More

In his Foreword to Keith Critchlow's *Islamic Patterns*, Seyyed Hossein Nasr explained that the geometrical basis of Islamic art is a means of relating multiplicity to unity by mathematical forms seen not as mental abstractions but as reflections of the celestial archetypes within both the cosmos and the soul of man. Like the mandala, sacred geometry leads one to the experience of unity within the cosmos and oneself, uniting the inner and outer into an inseparable whole. Critchlow's work illustrates in the complex language of geometry the relationship between the parts and the whole.

John Michell in *City of Revelation* described a sacred canon of proportion that appears to have existed in pre-Celtic Britain, in ancient Greece and Egypt, in Israel and Iran, and later in Christian Europe—a canon reflecting the relationships underlying geometry and music, the same ones underlying the universe. Archetypal temple plans appear to have utilized the relationships described in the canon.

Michell's last book, with Alan Brown, published in 2009, is *How the World Is Made: The Story of Creation According to Sacred Geometry*. In part 1 he pointed out that although it may not seem important what story we use to explain the universe, it really is crucial because our understanding determines our attitude toward life and "how we experience it." The geometrical and numerical aspect of nature is the subject of his book:

> At the root of these geometrical studies, and developed through them, is a worldview that is very different from the scientific version. It fulfils all that is required of a cosmology, being in accord with our physical knowledge of the universe, but describing it as an organic whole—as the macrocosm or large-scale counterpart of its microcosm, the human mind. It is that constant, ever-recurring picture of the world which has many names and symbols—the perennial philosophy, the cosmic canon, divine law, the heavenly city, the garden of paradise,

the philosopher's stone, the holy grail. Behind all these images is a central core of knowledge which is true at all times. It sanctifies the individual in whom it is established, and its periods of social influence are times of justice and the rebirth of culture.[10]

Contrasting and contradictory theories of origins of the universe abound, Michell wrote, drawn from the same scientific data, each theory with expert adherents of similar education. "One thing we do know, not just from the ancient philosophers but from common observation, is that the world is reflexive and responds to however we choose or are taught to imagine it. . . . You can choose whichever model you like, and the consequences will follow."[11] Synchronicity, everyday coincidences, Michell saw as illustrations of a reflexive universe.

Traditional people understand creation of the universe to begin with the One and to descend through multiple states of being. In *The Sense of Unity* Ardalan and Bakhtiar provide a table of geometric forms with some of their meanings. For example, nature is represented by a five-pointed figure or star that is related to the elements (ether, air, fire, water, earth) and the five senses. Geometric forms appearing in art and architecture can be "read" for their symbolic meanings, as can be further explored through the work of Keith Critchlow. In his elegant books, including *Order in Space* and *Time Stands Still*, Critchlow presents intricate drawings of "order as pattern." A careful study of his work can yield an understanding of some of the subtle meanings expressed in the use of various geometric forms.

In *Sacred Geometry* Nigel Pennick wrote that "Geometry exists everywhere in nature: its order underlies the structure of all things from molecules to galaxies, from the smallest virus to the largest whale."[12] Doczi's book *The Power of Limits* shows this through page after page of intricate drawings.

Science, Geometry, Pattern and Proportion, Encoding, and More

The geometric figures shown by Ardalan and Bakhtiar are related to number, and number has accrued many symbolic meanings. For example, 1 is the Creator; 2, the intellect and descent from unity and all pairs of corresponding opposites; 3, the soul or the symbol of God or fertility in nature; 4, matter, the solid earth, and the four humors; 5, nature or the pentagram matched to the extremities of the human body, the five senses, the virgin, symbol of eternal rather than created things; 6, the body, the six directions; 7, the universe; 8, qualities or symbol of the element earth; 9, beings of this world—plant, animal, mineral; 10, the holy tetractys or the created universe; 12, the zodiac, the twelve body orifices, and as Lawlor called it, the mother of life; 28, the stations of the moon and number of vertebrae; 360, the number of solar days and veins in the body. These are only a few of the potential meanings of numbers, gleaned from John Michell's *The Dimensions of Paradise* and from Ardalan and Bakhtiar's *The Sense of Unity*.

Michell's *How the World Is Made* goes into considerable detail about the geometry of number. One is symbol of the universe, while the structural numbers and geometries occurring in the architecture of the universe are 4 and 8 and 3 and 6, with the geometry of 12 embracing them all. The numbers 5 and 10 pertain to life and growth. The number 7 is the number of the soul, 9 of the mysteries, while 11 mediates between sublunary 10 and heavenly 12. The number 12 is very significant to Michell; he calls it the number of Universal Order and Harmony. The pattern of the heavens is based on 12, according to Michell, while Atlantis was "mistakenly" founded upon the number 10—the main reason, he wrote, that it failed.

You may enjoy reading more on geometry and number and learning to see evidence of pattern and proportion in nature.

Science, Geometry, Pattern and Proportion, Encoding, and More

Gematria is a language in which the assigned numerical values of letters in a word are added together to translate its hidden meaning, an additional convention being that words of equal numerical value may be substituted. This is one form of encoding.

Idries Shah's *The Sufis* contains accounts of numerical Abjad coding; students learn what numbers are assigned to letters. Shah gives as an example the Persian poet Attar's name, meaning "the chemist" or "seller of perfumes." Decoded, this gives the number 280. Restoring the numbers to "their order of greatness (hundreds, then tens)," this converts to 200 + 80, which represent the essence RF. Shah says that in Arabic RF stands for "the fluttering of a bird," suggesting *The Parliament of the Birds (The Conference of the Birds)*, Attar's most famous work. Other implications are intuition, the movement exercises of the dervish, and a "plant allegory because Sufism is of a growing, adaptive, organic and necessary nature, according to its followers."[13]

Nigel Pennick's *Magical Alphabets* presents some of the meanings attributed to letters in a number of different traditions.

Many spiritual texts are written in code. There is one meaning comprehended by the literalists. But sometimes there are very different meanings for those who know how to decipher the encoding or are able to understand more subtle meanings. Things are not always as they first appear.

The contemporary translations of Neal Douglas-Klotz, as in *The Hidden Gospel*, based on his studies of Aramaic—thought to have been the language Jesus spoke—express very different understandings from the usual King James version of what Jesus said: connotations as well as denotations are given, based on the original language used. "Words slip and slide," as T. S. Eliot wrote, and it is important to become aware of very different meanings that come through different translators and interpreters, and especially to be aware of other versions when we are confronted by individuals whose understandings of spiritual texts are limited to the only ones they know—often literal ones, based on single translations. Many spiritual texts have a number of levels of meaning, each to be understood at a different level of consciousness, and with sometimes very different meanings.

Computer programs have made possible the depiction of fractals based on complex mathematical equations. What is fascinating about these images is the similarity they show to what appears in nature. Jeff Berkowitz wrote, "If we are now able to construct natural objects like mountains, hills, trees, planets, etc., using our truly simple computational tools, imagine what the Divine Presence is able to accomplish with tools we can scarcely imagine. The incredible depth of the orchestration of life in the universe is truly awesome and overwhelming."[14]

With Mandelbrot images, further magnification yields ever smaller replicas, seemingly never ending and beyond our capacity to know or measure. A shoreline, that on a map may appear as a straight line, is shown to have myriad intricacies, as further magnified inlets appear with tinier and tinier permutations.

What most people know about chaos theory is the butterfly effect—the idea that something as seemingly insignificant as the fluttering of a butterfly's wings can affect weather across the world. James Gleick wrote, "In science as in life, it is well known that a chain of events can have a point of crisis that could magnify small changes. But chaos meant that such points were everywhere."[15]

Chaos theory is a clear message of interconnectedness in our world, one that has extremely important ramifications in all that we do, individually as well as collectively.

From what appears to be chaos, meaningful coincidences—what Michell saw as evidence of a reflexive universe—do

Science, Geometry, Pattern and Proportion, Encoding, and More

seem to occur. The Sufis say, "If you take one step toward God, He takes ten toward you." Synchronicity seems to me to have to do with a person's spiritual awareness and openness to notice signs when they appear. The more often one is able to do this, the more often meaningful signs seem to appear. Capacity is opened to be able to receive messages from the universe.

Physicist David Bohm formed a hypothesis about reality that echoes for me in current terms what the Sufi master Muhyiddin Ibn 'Arabi (1165–1240) wrote. As I understand what Ibn 'Arabi and Bohm say, it is that there is a Unity (in Arabic *Haqq*, meaning Truth for Ibn 'Arabi) from which all comes. From this Unity comes the world of primary reality, the implicate order (*batin*, the inner)—the "real" reality behind the forms that we know in our world. From primary reality comes secondary reality, the explicate order (*zahir*, the outer), which is the world of duality that we know and love. This is the world of manifestation in which we live our lives on earth, but this world of forms comes from and returns to the implicate order, which some might think of as the world of archetypes. By now we know from modern physics that this solid-seeming secondary reality world in which we live is not solid, that what seems to us as solid is mostly empty space ("cloudy, cloudy is the stuff of stones," as Richard Wilbur wrote in "Epistemology" in *Ceremony and Other Poems*). So we are already "not in Kansas anymore" and have an inkling that the world is a mysterious place and that the invisible world is immensely powerful and present.

In an experiment named for Ernst Chladni, sand is put on a metal plate and a note is played, as by a violin, in a way that will resonate with the plate. A pattern forms in the sand. When a different note is played, a different pattern appears. The resonant field is not where the sand gathers but where there is "empty" space. The invisible space, sometimes spoken of as the "silence," is full of potential creative power. What is invisible to us is the source of the pattern that we see.

British biologist Rupert Sheldrake has developed an earlier hypothesis of formative causation by organizing fields of force that are called morphic or morphogenetic fields. These may be understood in somewhat the same way as Doczi's power of limits ("limit gives form to the limitless. This is the power of limits."). Morphogenetic fields encode the basic patterns that are repeated in organisms. Another idea of Sheldrake's is that there are not laws of nature so much as habits of nature that are subject to change when the fields affecting them change.

Morphic resonance is a term now used to describe the increasing ease with which new skills are learned as larger numbers acquire them. Sheldrake has written extensively about this phenomenon, which in popular parlance is sometimes referred to as the 100th monkey factor.

In *Lifetide* Lyall Watson wrote that on a Pacific island a monkey took a sweet potato down to the shore to wash it free of sand. Other monkeys on the island saw this and began to do the same until a critical number (arbitrarily known as the 100th monkey) had washed their sweet potatoes. At that point a threshold appeared to have been reached and monkeys on islands with no contact with the first island also began to do the same. How could this happen? Rupert Sheldrake's hypothesis would seem to explain this tale.

This 100th monkey idea has been adopted by many to give hope to those who feel that their small actions cannot make much difference in the crises of our world. The idea is that if a small but critical number of people do some action or think some thought, that action or thought will spread much farther, even exponentially. This is the idea behind Transcendental Meditation's claim that meditators in a city can bring down a crime rate.

And it is behind the idea of group prayer. Larry Dossey, MD, has written about the apparent effectiveness of group prayer—at a distance—in bettering the conditions of patients in studies undertaken at San Francisco General Hospital. It is interesting to dowse the aura of a group before and after a concentrated effort such as a prayer, for the group aura is very much larger after the effort, which may be simply one of directed attention without any religious context. In anecdotal evidence for the effectiveness of prayer groups, usually no distinction is made about the level of clarity or ability of the individuals involved, which is no doubt disturbing to scientists looking for more rigor in the details, and I do know from our own experience that the level of ability or awareness of individuals and their degree of centeredness make considerable difference. Also, Dossey concluded that prayers without request for a specific outcome but with the sense of "Thy will be done" seemed the most successful.

Sheldrake's anecdotal backup to the morphic resonance idea includes examples from the growing ease in creating crystals in laboratories to the increasing numbers of birds learning to peck out lids on milk bottles, rats running mazes more quickly than their predecessors did, the clusters of scientific "discoveries" that seem to occur once a breakthrough is made. I know how much easier it is for people to learn to dowse now that more people have learned; as a skill dowsing is no longer understood to be limited to the seventh son of a seventh son.

If Sheldrake's morphic resonance hypothesis is true, and it certainly seems to have validity, it also changes how we look at a lot of things. It might not be necessary for people to have had physical contact for aspects of their cultures to be disseminated. We already know that it is virtually impossible to create an experiment in which the mindset of the experimenters is not part of the result, calling the result into some

Science, Geometry, Pattern and Proportion, Encoding, and More

question. And it seems that other "sure" ways we have had of evaluating, such as the understanding that physical contact is essential for diffusion, also need to be reexamined.

Once even partial impact of what the geometry, number, pattern, and proportion that appear in nature, along with all the rest of what science so far has hypothesized, begin to register, our sense of wonder can only grow, as must our sense that there is meaning and purpose and interconnection in everything that is. As through science we gradually become aware of still further complexities and of the discovered greater vastness of the universe, far beyond what previously had been known and even now understood as beyond human comprehension, our wonder and humility can only increase.

The more veils that are lifted, the more we become aware of still other veils that remain. We human beings are not the center of the universe, but we are part of it all, and we do have a role to play.

3

THE MUSIC OF THE SPHERES

MUSIC ALSO is based on pattern and proportion. In *The Secret Power of Music* David Tame mentioned that Gary Peacock found that "the relationships in the periodic table of elements, from which all matter is formed, resemble the overtone structure in music.... In other words: matter is music."[1]

Tame also referred to Doczi's *The Power of Limits* and his detailing of similarities between ratios and proportions found in various branches of science. Music is not included in Doczi's book, but Tame wrote,

> Quite simply, *all* of the data in his book, which links physics with biology with astronomy with architecture and so forth, can be explained in terms of music, but this would open up too vast a subject in itself. Nevertheless, his book is inherently associated with the principles of music from cover to cover. The ratios which in music are known as the fifth and fourth intervals occur again and again throughout nature.... Some leaves... reveal... counterpoint in the ratios and proportions to which the veins are arranged to the left and to the right of the stem.[2]

In *Nada Brahma: The World Is Sound* Joachim-Ernst Berendt wrote of knowing through photo-acoustic spectroscopy of the sounds that a rose makes when it bursts into bloom and that all the corn stalks in a field also make sounds. Research has also shown that "plants in a meadow, field, or forest will wither if their vibrations (in other words, their sounds) relate disharmonically to other plants in the vicinity."[3] Suggestions for companion planting—which plants will grow happily together and seem to help each other and which seem to stunt each other's growth—probably mirror this finding.

Berendt wrote, "The science of harmonics knows that any form of organic life—a fish, a flower, a leaf, a fruit, a beetle, any creature at all—*is* sound, that in fact even the 'most beautiful' forms of the inorganic world, the crystals, *are* sound."[4]

Citro wrote that "The basic codes that direct molecules and govern bodies are music, but they are infrasound which we cannot hear."[5]

In the experiments of Ernst Chladni, as mentioned before, sand was scattered on steel disks and notes played on a violin. Patterns formed in the sand, with different notes bringing forth different patterns.

Anthroposophist Doctor Hans Jenny continued this work, scattering "disks with liquids, metal filings and powders." In *Tuning the Human Instrument*, Steven Halpern wrote that Jenny "controlled for the variables of a violin bow by using the definite calibrations of a vibrating crystal. . . . As the pitch ascended the musical scale, the harmonic patterns on the disks also changed . . . but not just to the previously discovered geometries. Many of the evoked images were 'organic' shapes, such as the . . . hexagonal cells of honeycombs, the vanishing spirals of the nautilus, and many more."[6]

In *The Third Ear* Joachim-Ernst Berendt wrote that

> Jenny has shown that the patterns he obtains . . . exactly correspond to nature's own preferred forms—in the development of fleecy clouds and the formation of sand dunes, in the shells of mussels and snails, in the structures of sea- and lake-beds caused by the movement of water, in foam, in ostrich and peacock feathers, in snake skins and skeletons, in coral shapes and seed-capsules, and in blossoms and leaves.[7]

Jenny used the same procedure to show visible patterns within some of the great music of the West.

If beings are sound, then health is harmony, and sound is one of the ways that harmony may be restored. There is great interest in this field and many books and CDs explore aspects of sound healing. These range from instruction in toning to choices of music. *Sound Health: The Music and Sounds That Make Us Whole*, by Steven Halpern with Louis Savary, studies the effects of sound and music on body, mind, and spirit and shows how to develop a "diet of sound" that nurtures all of these.

The Mozart Effect by Don Campbell includes accounts by musicians, doctors, shamans, and health care professionals who use music in therapeutic ways. Students who sing or play an instrument score significantly higher on SATs than those who do not. Campbell reveals how lifelong exposure to sound can affect learning and memory. There are exercises in his book as well as descriptions of fifty common ailments for which he says music can effect amelioration or cure. Sound healers help by supplying what is missing in the individual's soundscape.

Learning overtone singing is said to change your hearing and enlarge your perception of reality, tune your chakras, and cleanse your energy system. Around the world Jill Purce has offered workshops in the power of "the healing voice" to reconnect us to the "resonant world" and to heal and transform.

When asked to look at a group of Benedictine monks suffering with depression and exhaustion, Alfred Tomatis found that a return to their usual pattern of chanting six to eight hours a day, that had been discontinued prior to the start of their malaise, was what they needed for their return to health.

The principles of cymatics have a contemporary use in vibrational medicine. Peter Guy Manners, a British medical doctor, developed Cymatics Therapy, using a toning device to transmit the signature vibrations of healthy tissues and organs. The idea is to play back to the cells those vibrations needed to re-entrain them. Sonopuncture or sound acupuncture is another technique that has been used to mitigate pain.

In *The Secret Power of Music* David Tame wrote that modern research has shown that most functions of the body can be affected by musical tones, both by direct effect on the cells and organs and indirectly by effect on the emotions. A teenage fad was to take eggs to rock concerts and place them on the stage, where they would seem to become hard-boiled by midway through the concerts. What may have been happening in the bodies of the people in the audience was not considered. Research has shown that rock music is bad for digestion, dangerous while driving, and that it raises blood pressure.

People are affected by sound, but so are other life forms. Dorothy Retallack studied the effects of various kinds of music on plants and wrote about this in *The Sound of Music and Plants*. She found that within a month those petunias that had been exposed to rock music died. Experiments in Canada and the Soviet Union showed that wheat treated with sound grew larger, was more frost-tolerant, and yielded more grain. Another experiment showed that the Bach Brandenburg Concertos helped geraniums to grow faster. In evaluating effects, "good" music was considered to be what gave life, "bad" music what brought death.

In *Secrets of the Soil* Peter Tompkins and Christopher Bird suggested that birdsong at dawn opens the stomata of plants to receive nutrients. Dan Carlson developed Sonic Bloom, a foliar fertilizing spray to be applied with a "combination of frequencies and harmonics exactly accordant with the pre-dawn bird concerts that continue past sunup into morning."[8] Hindu ragas fit this requirement but were not welcome to some Western ears. Carlson then enlisted the help of a music

The Music of the Spheres

teacher, Michael Holtz, who looked for Western music in this sonic range and found it in Vivaldi and Bach. Holtz investigated birdsong and "began to feel that God had created the birds for more than just freely flying about and warbling. Their very singing must somehow be intimately linked to the mysteries of seed germination and plant growth."[9] And he became aware of the weakening of this linkage through the depredations of DDT and other hazards.

In *Secrets of the Soil* Tompkins and Bird reported Viktor Schauberger's account of hearing a farmer singing a scale into a barrel of water as he tossed in bits of soil while stirring clockwise and counterclockwise with a wooden spoon. This product was then sprinkled on the fields after planting and near Eastertide. Sound was a crucial element in this effort.

The soundscapes in which we live have definite effects upon all of us. Berendt points out that noise is the opposite of sound and that the fullness of sound is silence. One learns through meditation that "silence" is full of all possibilities, and gradually, as one spends more and more time in silence, one may begin to hear something of "the music of the spheres." David Tame wrote that the word *anahata* refers not only to omnipresent cosmic sound, but in Sanskrit is the name of the heart chakra that is considered to be the anchoring point of the Word of God within the human being. There will be more about the heart in a chapter later on.

Australian Aborigines follow "songlines" to find their way in the trackless desert. People studying shamanic plant spirit medicine often speak of the songs of the various plants contacted. A Native American flute player suggested looking to the landscape to suggest what to play—learning to play the landscape—instead of thinking in terms of our usual Western ways with notes. Paul Winter and others incorporate the songs of wolves and other creatures in their compositions. Many tapes and CDs record the music of oceans and streams, rain and lightning, songbirds and frogs. A giant wind harp once stood on a Vermont hill and an LP was made of its sound. We are surrounded by the beautiful music of nature and are very fortunate if we live where we are able to hear it.

4

LIGHT

IN MANY ways—in religions, folktales, epics, popular literature, political rhetoric—we think of and replay a battle between light and darkness that is usually understood as meaning a battle between good (the light) and evil (the darkness). It is well, however, to remember the necessity of the dark as contrast, making the light appear more radiant, and of the dark night of the soul and the via negativa that may birth the light of understanding. And in *The Man of Light in Iranian Sufism* Henry Corbin wrote of the "black light" that is "the light of the pure Essence in its ipseity, in its abscondity; the ability to perceive it depends on a spiritual state described as 'reabsorption in God.'"[1] This black light is understood to signal the threshold to the highest awareness. Citro wrote of the black light that is "the inner energy of matter and the secret light that the alchemists hoped to find. Black because it is invisible and the true color of light is black."[2]

At the winter solstice we celebrate the turning of the seasonal tide, the time after which there is a little more daylight each day, and we do this with fire—candles and bonfires and yule logs—to encourage the sun in a sort of "as below, so above" reversal. Near the solstice also come Chanukah, the Jewish festival of light, and Christmas, the celebration of the birth of the child that Christians believe brought the light of God to a dark world.

Many scriptures say that God is light. In the King James version of the Bible there are:

Light

> The LORD is my light and my salvation. (Psalm 27:1)
>
> The LORD shall be unto thee an everlasting light. (Isaiah 60:19)
>
> In him was life; and the life was the light of men. (John 1:4)
>
> This then is the message which we have heard of him, and declare unto you, that God is light. (1 John 1:5)
>
> The light of the body is the eye: therefore when thine eye is single, thy whole body also is full of light. (Luke 11:34)

The Buddha, dying, is supposed to have said, "Make of yourself a light." And in the Qur'an it is said, "Allah is the light of heaven and earth."

Suhrawardi (1155–1191), an alchemist and a Sufi, aware of the teachings of Pythagoras and Plotinus as well as those of Zarathustra and Hermes, is known for his philosophy of illumination by the pure light. He wrote, "All comes from Allah as light waves spread from the sun." In this paradigm there are levels of light, the first below Allah being Creative Light, with each level of light less as the light gets farther and farther away. There is divine light within the human being, and through the spiritual battle with the ego self, through discipline, contemplation, and prayers, that light may become manifest.

In *The Man of Light in Iranian Sufism* Henry Corbin referred to Phos as the archetype of the man of light: Phos speaks through Mary Magdalene in the *Pistis Sophia*, considered to be the testament of the religion of the man of light. To actualize this body of light within oneself, one works to unfold the resurrection body with its supersensory senses. These are senses more subtle than those we are accustomed to using that can function here but are needed to function in the world of Hurqalya, the celestial earth beyond this world described in that tradition. The temple of light that the human being can become is his/her resurrection body, developed with finer chakras called latifas, each of which is associated

Light

with a color and with the realization exemplified by one of the prophets. Many practices taught by the Sufis have as their intention the realizations that bring about the unfoldment of this resurrection body while the individual is still living on the earth. The heart is considered to be the subtle center of light, and in a later chapter there will be more about the importance of the heart.

To understand some of these concepts it seems helpful to go again to David Bohm, who is reported to have called matter "frozen light" and to have said that light may be the primary reality and space the landscaping of it. You will recall that Bohm's secondary reality is the world as we experience it, but primary reality is the more real reality and is that from which secondary reality comes. And beyond primary reality is the Unity from which all originates.

Peter Russell's *From Science to God: The Mystery of Consciousness and the Meaning of Light* was published in 2002, but I just read it and thought it timely reading, especially remembering Nasr's words included at the beginning of this book. After studying the scientific mystery of light and realizing that consciousness is fundamental to the cosmos and the bridge that allows for an understanding of "a universe in which science and spirit no longer conflict," Russell's perceptions of reality radically changed. He wrote, "God is often said to be the creator and source of all creation. So is consciousness. . . . Consciousness is the source and creator of everything we know."[3]

So we have some consensus for the idea of God as Light, the work needed to actualize the light dormant within the human being, the world of primary reality as a world of light of higher or finer quality than the light of this world, light's relationship to consciousness, and the relationship of consciousness to God.

Angels or winged beings of light populate religious and shamanic tales and art from around the world. Peter Lamborn

Wilson's *Angels* in the original hardcover (and abridged as *Angels: Messengers of the Gods* as part of the Art and Imagination series) is a fine overview of widespread and longtime belief in, and the art depicting, angelic beings.

Angels have become a very popular subject in our time, with many books alleging contact with angelic beings who assist in healing and with other needs.

In *The Physics of Angels: Exploring Where Science and Spirit Meet* there is a dialogue between theologian Matthew Fox and biologist Rupert Sheldrake based on the writings of several Christian mystics. Sheldrake wrote,

> The gods in polytheistic religions are assimilated into monotheism by being treated as angels. If the many gods are recognized as subject to the one supreme God, they can be accepted as divine intermediaries and as divine powers. The difference between monotheism and polytheism, at first sight so stark, is softened and modified by the recognition of the angels.[4]

Later he wrote of understanding angels in a new way.

> Nature is organized by fields, and these fields are the realms of activity that bind and order the energy or power. If divine power flows through and into all things, if it is the energy of all things, and if it is channeled through the angels, then the fields that give this power its differentiated forms are associated with consciousness and intelligence. The angels are, as it were, the consciousness of the fields operating at all levels of nature, as in the flow of the winds and in the powers of living beings such as animals. The generative powers of nature are associated with intelligence.[5]

Of Thomas Aquinas and similarities in the descriptions of the movement of angels with that of "photons and other quantum particles in quantum theory," Sheldrake wrote that "I think the parallels arise because he's dealing with the same question: How can something nonmaterial and indivisible move and act on bodies located in particular places?"[6]

Light

Sheldrake commented that in the Middle Ages and before that time it was thought that the cosmos was alive and populated with innumerable conscious beings.

> We now have a completely different, vastly larger, and much more creative cosmology than they had in the Middle Ages. The angels of such a cosmos are very mysterious indeed. We have hardly begun to try to understand how their conscious powers may be related to the evolution of nature, to the development of humanity, or to the expansion of human consciousness. We know next to nothing about the superhuman intelligences that influence our lives.[7]

The message of their book is that angels exist in astronomical numbers, have been present from the origin of the universe, are the governing intelligences of nature, have a special relationship to human consciousness, and inspire, protect, bring messages, and guide. Questions for the future include how to understand the consciousness of aspects of the cosmos and whether new species of angels are coming into being with our evolving world.

In their book Fox and Sheldrake bring a fascinating new dimension to angelology and toward understanding those wondrous beings of light. But now back to secondary reality—the world as we usually experience it.

John Ott experimented with colored lights on plants, animals, human beings, and cells, using time-lapse microphotography. From this work he learned the importance of full-spectrum natural light and developed lighting systems for homes and businesses. Ott's books, *Health and Light* and *Light, Radiation, and You: How to Stay Healthy*, describe the effects of natural and artificial light on living beings. Full-spectrum lights improve indoor plant growth and have been shown to help people with seasonal affective disorder.

Ott felt that for good health people need to spend time outdoors without glasses in sunlight. I note that recent studies indicating the value of vitamin D3 are accompanied by some doctors now recommending a short time spent in full noon sunlight without sunscreen, which seems to be a significant change from recently past medical directives.

In ancient Thebes and Karnak there were said to be color halls for research, and other societies explored color healing also, so this is not a new idea. Richard Gerber wrote, "The priests of ancient Egypt, Babylonia, and China used color or colored light in many of their healing practices. Sunlight therapy was a common medical practice in historic Greek, Chinese and Roman times."[8]

In *Light: Medicine of the Future*, Jacob Liberman wrote of a coming revolution in medical care based on gentler, less invasive treatment with light. In his preface he also mentioned a discovery he made in 1975 while developing a vision-improvement system. He noticed that people who were always looking for some particular thing in life missed everything else. He hypothesized that "if we looked at nothing, perhaps we would see everything." He experimented in his own life. "In addition to expanding my field of vision, reducing my nearsightedness, improving my eyesight, reducing pain, and changing my point of view, it allowed me to see things that I never previously saw or even thought existed."[9] These included auras and the visible energy in air. Later he found that this soft glance could be used as a scanning tool that would tell him where a problem was in a patient's body. He felt that vision was meant to be used in this effortless way. This soft glance is a valuable way of adding to our awareness of the world and is one taught as part of some meditations. It is also the sight with which some are able to "see" beings from other dimensions. It is interesting that this appears to be the kind of vision that an infant first has.

Healing with light and color are aspects of contemporary vibrational medicine. Richard Gerber, MD, is the author of

Vibrational Medicine: New Choices for Healing Ourselves and *Vibrational Medicine for the 21st Century: The Complete Guide to Energy Healing and Spiritual Transformation*. The second book includes a color and light-healing resource guide, a chapter with a history of many different forms of color and light therapy, and an overview of current modalities. These include ocular light therapy (projection of a colored light into the eyes), colorpuncture (stimulation of acupoints and meridians), reflexology light therapy (projection of colored light onto the foot zone corresponding to the problem area in the body), and channeling of colors by a healer. Gerber also mentions color-breathing, in which a person can visualize breathing in specific colors directed to the chakras. Gerber says that British color therapist Pauline Willis suggests that people imagine differently colored leaves or flowers to help in this.

Another imagery exercise is to visualize taking into your body a specific color targeted to treat a specific area and problem.

Gabriel Cousens, MD, wrote *Spiritual Nutrition and the Rainbow Diet* to promote the idea of choosing foods with color to resonate with and feed color energy to the chakras. Andrew Weil, MD, also suggests among his food recommendations the choosing of foods with color for therapeutic reasons. Doctor Cousens recommends starting the day with red-orange-yellow foods and moving up the spectrum during the day.

Much has been published about the choices of color in clothing and home furnishings for therapeutic reasons. For example, Willis suggests blue clothes to help lower blood pressure and red socks and mittens for cold feet and hands. She says that silk and 100 percent cotton, dyed with natural dyes, should be used for therapeutic clothing. Warm colors tend to enliven, cool colors to calm.

Light

The Gerber chapter mentioned would be my suggestion for starting to read in this area. Be aware that books on color are not consistent in how they range and interpret colors. Parts of the chakra system are also given different colors in different traditions: for example, the heart center may be thought of as green or gold, depending on the system. But red, orange, yellow, green, blue, indigo, violet is the usual range, starting with the base chakra and rising to the crown.

Dowsers have used colored gels with lights and photographs for timed sending of colors to individuals, when permission has been received and if dowsed as appropriate. But, just as one can move beyond ingesting a plant substance to requesting help from a plant, there is another way to ask for help from light and color.

Toward the end of his earth life Terry Ross was asking Light to do the healing for which his prayers were requested. This Light did not travel by the speed of light, as does that in this world, but was instantaneous, so it was Light from beyond this world. Terry would dowse what color a patient needed to receive and also frequently used a peach-colored ray as a carrier for his healing prayers.

In prayers in many traditions it is requested that human beings or creatures be held in the light. A traditional Irish blessing says, "May the blessing of light be on you, light without and light within. . . . And may the light shine out of the two eyes of you, like a candle set in the two windows of a house, bidding the wanderer come in out of the storm."

In meditation one may explore the effects of visualizing light and color. Those suffering with seasonal affective disorder may want to investigate practices to increase the light within as a way of helping themselves. With our glance we may learn to project light to others, a Sufi spiritual practice that is also suggested in the Irish Christian blessing. Photisms of light, lights of various colors spontaneously arising, are said to accompany certain spiritual levels or insights, and Terry Ross felt that flashes of light often accompanied spontaneous healings.

We all have the possibility of developing the colors and brilliance of our auras, but great beings have a bioluminescence that more easily may be seen or dowsed. We were amazed once to dowse the remembrance of the aura of Pir Vilayat Inayat Khan, still strong in a meditation tent in which he had not physically been for many months.

5
Earth

THE GAIA hypothesis developed by James Lovelock has given many people a new sense of what our ancestors felt—that the earth is a living being, our "mother," by some thought of as an angel, but in all cases a being that must be honored and treated well if there are not to be dire consequences for earth's inhabitants. If a self-regulating being, the earth can throw off harmful influences, including human beings. We have not been treating earth well, as becomes more and more disturbingly clear, and although many concerned individuals have tried to bring to wider awareness the harm that human beings have been doing to our earth home, with disastrous potential consequences for all of us, the message gets lost amid other concerns that seem to some people more immediate.

One of the less well-known but important areas in which we have been harming the earth is in being oblivious to nature's ways. Instead of understanding that whole nature is our textbook, we have tried to substitute our very limited understanding of parts and our mistaken ideas of control. Finally some attention is being paid to work like that described in *Biomimicry: Innovation Inspired by Nature* by Janine M. Benyus, where the way nature does things is being studied so that similar methods can be adapted for human use. A PBS Nova program (February 9, 2011) on "smart materials" featured recent inventions based on a study of nature. One example was a plastic, configured with a raised pattern suggested by a study of shark skin, that has been shown to be far less conducive to the growth of bacteria than is plain plastic.

This discovery, based on observation of nature, shows great potential for use in hospitals, where the growth of harmful bacteria has become a serious and life-threatening problem.

William McDonough and Michael Braungart have written about nature's abundance. They applaud commerce that applies nature's ways so that there is nourishment for something new after each useful life. This is a large step beyond the usual understanding of recycling, for they write of the creation of products that can be returned to the biosphere or the technosphere. Organic food packaging, for example, can be returned to the soil, while aspects of technical metabolism can be designed to circulate within closed-loop industrial cycles. Excerpts of the writing of McDonough and Braungart are included in *Choices for Sustainable Living*, published by the Northwest Earth Institute.

Around the world individuals and groups are trying to help people to think more deeply about environmental issues. Where I live, the Vermont (now known as Catamount) Earth Institute has made publications of the Northwest Earth Institute available for library discussion groups, aiming to help people to develop voluntary simplicity and sustainable living practices. Another topic in the series is *Discovering a Sense of Place*. If we understand that we are where we are for a reason, then it is important to discover what that reason is (dowsing is a fine tool to help in this discovery) and to learn as much as we can about where we are. This may include the history of former inhabitants and their land use, but there is much more to it than that. What is the topography of the land? Where are the watersheds? What are the native animals and plants? And, as most do not yet consider, what are the earth energies, and what does the land want to happen here?

Land will respond to intent. Where clean-up and ordering occur, the feeling of lightening on the land is heartening. And no matter how much we have already done, we all need to do more about recycling—or better yet, encouraging the creation of products that can be returned to the biosphere or technosphere—and we need to learn how to create less waste, while making more order in our lives.

If your intent toward the bird and animal kingdoms is that of a friend, then many creatures will come where you are. Attention paid to plants and trees will be rewarded.

Attention to the plant world also means attention to the soil, and an important book to read on this subject is *Secrets of the Soil* by Peter Tompkins and Christopher Bird. In it they describe many different approaches to caring for the soil, but although it is not said overtly, consciousness and intent seem to be crucial factors.

To produce one inch of topsoil is said to take 500 years. Topsoil needs to be cherished and protected.

In gardening, chemical fertilizers and insecticides are not the way to go. They are not part of nature's design or balance and cause many known problems and no doubt many more not yet known. Even so-called safe products have downsides, and the effects of products are usually not truly known for a very long time. Just think of the frequent changes in what we are told about what medicines are considered to be safe! And whenever we attempt to eradicate what is considered a "pest" from the human point of view, we disrupt the natural food chain with its checks and balances. As a species we are much too ignorant of subtle relationships to be making such drastic decisions. There is a better way.

Whatever state nature is now in, we are all part of nature and all in it together. A view has been that human sin is the root of most evil. But in my understanding of the Sufi tradition, sin is not thought of as "original sin" that all assume at birth, but rather as a lack of knowledge or awareness, and especially as forgetfulness of what the human role in the world is intended to be: a bridge between heaven and earth, as a "transformer of subtle energies," steward of the earth and caregiver for God's creation.

Many folklore traditions refer to a past when all creatures were herbivores and it was humankind that broke this gentler pattern and brought about the eating of meat and the preying of one creature upon another. A question is, does nature sometimes mirror the human being? There is a later chapter on the mirror.

Something else we may want to consider in relationship to harmony is that God's purposes may not always be what we in our finite selves can understand. From a lofty perspective, the purpose of our being in the world may well be as a transient time in which we are intended to get our acts in order and to become transformers of subtle energy in divine service. If this is our purpose in life on earth, it does not necessarily include our physical or material well-being, although it may include these. If, as we believe, we do go on after death—all beings and not just human beings—then what happens to our physical selves here is not as important as it would otherwise be. But what happens in our consciousness is much more important than it would otherwise be. If one believes this, it helps a great deal with the pain of both observing and experiencing misery. The great cosmic dance goes on—with forms materializing and then dissolving.

If the world is self-regulating, as the Gaia hypothesis suggests, ecological balance is required. This may mean that if there are too many human beings or too many lemmings, some may not be able to stay in manifestation. Some may not be meant to have their lives extended. The idea of karma helps some to accept this, but it is difficult to allow even faint understandings of this idea to penetrate, so conditioned are we to believe in the importance of progress against what we perceive as unnecessary harshness in the world. But it does often seem that as one early cause of death for human beings

Earth

is removed, another fills its place. Is this the self-regulatory process of Gaia? Stephen Harrod Buhner's *Plant Intelligence and the Imaginal Realm* includes much about this subject.

The intent of the Golden Rule of conduct, "Do unto others as you would have them do unto you," means to do what we can in service to God—or the Whole or however one wants to conceptualize this—through help to our fellow beings and our earth home, and this seems a clear direction. Yet *How Can I Help?* by Ram Dass and Paul Gorman reminds us that knowing what is true help is not always simple. Becoming aware of our interconnection with everyone and everything, learning to truly listen and to be a witness, and opening ourselves to *be* in our full humanity are all part of the process of preparing ourselves to be of service. And once again I suggest that learning to dowse is an excellent way to ask the questions about what help in a particular situation is appropriate.

6
EARTH ENERGIES

GEOMANCY IS a name given to the awakening of consciousness to "the process of bringing human activities into harmony and resonance with the earth and with the cosmos. It particularly relates to mankind's building activities on this earth and how they influence and affect the subtle electromagnetic currents that are everywhere present in the earth."[1] Geomancy implies learning how to do the right thing in the right place at the right time.

In the East the most well-known form of geomancy is called *feng shui* (meaning wind and water). There are differing schools of training, and many have tried to bring aspects of these complicated systems to the West (one glance at a picture of a Lo Pan compass will give some idea of the complexities involved). The purpose of feng shui is to make sure that the earth currents (the white tiger and the azure dragon) flow freely. Feng shui is used in placement of graves to benefit both deceased and surviving family members and in many ways for placement both of buildings and of rooms and furniture within buildings. The ideal building site is considered to be one that is facing south, with a hill and trees behind it and a watercourse meandering in front of the site. Inside a house the currents also need to flow smoothly, so that the placement of rooms and furniture is important, and there are various symbolic ways to overcome stagnant energy.

The basic idea is that there are earth currents that flow through or over the earth and that where these currents are able to move smoothly and harmoniously everything is beautiful and people are happy. But when these pathways are blocked—usually because of something human beings have done, not understanding these energies—then there are unhappiness, accidents, and many problems.

An interest in earth currents has been gathering in the West since the 1920s with the work of Alfred Watkins, although he was not the first to notice alignments of sites. Watkins described an alignment as being five sites (not necessarily from the same historical period, since new structures were often built on old sacred sites) within a ten-mile straight line, and he called these alignments ley lines. In 1969 Guy Underwood, a dowser, described his understanding of further earth currents in his book *The Pattern of the Past*.

Alexander Thom's surveys show the amazingly accurate geometries of ancient stone circles. John Michell, Keith Critchlow, Nigel Pennick, John and Caitlin Matthews, Paul Devereux, Michael Poynder, and Arthur Versluis have also contributed to the recent literature on sacred sites and sacred geometry. Sig Lonegren has added the perspective of a dowser. Jim Swan has written about Native American sites, partly to help government personnel understand and honor the fact that there can be sacred sites without structures built upon them.

Dowsers discovered that many ley lines also have dowseable energy, which Terry Ross described as six-to-eight-foot-wide bands. These widths fluctuate according to various factors and times of the moon. Energy leys or E-leys are the names usually used for these dowseable lines. A power point is where at least one energy ley and a blind spring meet, although sacred space sometimes has multiple energy leys converging with a blind spring. These configurations of energies are often marked by structures, sometimes from different time periods when newer buildings have been built on traditional sites, but they also occur in places where there is no structure.

Earth Energies

Dowsers understand a blind spring to be a water dome. Water from deep in the earth moves toward the surface but is hindered, often by stone ledge. The water then spins out in an odd number of veins at different depths. These water veins (not the domes themselves) are what dowsers most often seek for wells because they are usually the purest water available.

By now many kinds of earth energies and a number of grid patterns have been identified, although all people do not use the same names or agree on all of these energies, depending on their training, experience, and mindsets. If one understands the earth to be a living being, as in the Gaia theory, then it is not surprising that there are a variety of earth currents with some seeming somewhat like acupuncture meridians. We hope gradually to come to understand more about subtle earth energies, as has happened with the subtle anatomy of the human being. Perhaps someday we will have the kind of detail now available for the human physical body, but of course even that is not yet fully known or understood.

The chapter on water will briefly mention problems with water veins under buildings, but these are not the only lines of force that we would do well to be able to identify.

What we call chi lines are curving lines of energy on the earth, which seem to be similar to the acupuncture meridians of the body. When these chi lines can run unobstructed, the air smells sweet and there is a feeling on them of well-being and happiness. Often, however, these lines are blocked, and if you dowse you may find that the source of the problem is many, even hundreds of miles away. One can learn to unblock these lines by staking them in a way similar to the way an acupuncturist uses a needle, but this is not work for a beginner since damage can be caused if this work is not done correctly. Sometimes these lines can be unblocked by thought alone when one has received the permissions. Visions from the invisible world, when and if they come, seem to appear on positive chi lines.

Negative (blocked) chi lines are harmful to health, especially when in proximity to water veins, and it would be good to consult a trained and competent dowser if you suspect that these are present where you live or work.

Another harmful earth energy is what we call psychic damage, the imprint left on the land by something terrible that has happened to some being there. You may feel this negative energy even if you are not a dowser or if you don't know what it is. In many cases this damage can be healed. A trained dowser can assist, but your intention—expressed in right relationship to the land and cleanup—also can help in the healing.

I have mentioned energy leys in connection with sacred sites. What we call energy leys seem to us to come in a variety of strengths, so that there are some energy leys, although less intense than those at sacred sites, that many of us may frequently encounter. On energy leys the energy seems to be neutral in that it will tend to send a person further along on the road on which he or she is already traveling. Energy leys are fine places for short-term meditation but sometimes are too powerful to stay on for a long time. If you have an energy ley on your property, identify a place for your own sacred site on it and treat it with respect. If you walk along some of the energy leys in this country, you may find standing stones, just as you do in Great Britain, Ireland, and other parts of the world.

In *The New View over Atlantis* John Michell says that the ley system is connected with a former code of mystical science based on energy streams and their part in the renewal of life, with traces left in esoteric traditions, mythology, folklore, customs, monuments, and cultures.

Please be aware that relearning about earth energies is a relatively new field of interest and that there is not worldwide consensus on how terms are used. In reading books and particularly those from abroad, it is well to pay attention to how terms are defined in order not to become confused.

Part of learning to live on the earth is learning the proper place for each kind of energy. For example, negative water-vein energy is fine as a site for a compost pile because it is a breaking-down energy. But you don't want it under your bed or favorite chair.

If you are enough intrigued by this section to want to learn more about this, please read *The Divining Mind* for basic dowsing instruction and *The Divining Heart* for more information about earth energies.

On your own land it is good to locate the omphalos, the umbilicus, the psychic central point of the property. From it you define your space and find that you have geomantically, according to Reshad Feild, everything that you need. The sacred world tree is at an omphalos, but every place has its own omphalos; often it is the hearth of the home. The idea is to identify a point that is sacred and around which everything circles.

In another way of thinking of this, each of us is an omphalos: "Whithersoe'er you stand that is holy ground."

In *The Earth Spirit* John Michell wrote about the High King's court at Tara in Ireland, "arranged as a microcosm of the heavens and the country as a whole, thus imprinting the kingdom with a sacred pattern and declaring as official policy the unsuppressible human ambition for paradise on earth." The High King sat in the center, understood as the center of the universe, thus "setting forth the pattern of cosmic harmony as the model for affairs on earth, and symbolizing the ancient idea that each individual is at the centre of his own universe and is therefore responsible for ordering it on true cosmological principles."[2]

In *The Ancient Science of Geomancy* Nigel Pennick told about the setting of boundaries, meaning the creation of a special place set aside in space and time from a surrounding undefined area. By defining space you are creating order.

In the past, in England, there was an annual beating of the bounds on what was called Rogation Sunday. People walked around the boundaries of their land, beating the earth or boundary markers with willow or hazel boughs to ground the energy and re-energize the space. Nigel Pennick's books *Earth Harmony* and *Practical Magic in the Northern Tradition*, and *Earth Rites* by Janet and Colin Bord, describe many of the ceremonies used by earlier inhabitants to mark and define their living areas.

Today there are ceremonies that you can follow or create for your own space. The idea is recognition that you are on a particular piece of land for a reason, that you are its custodian but that in that role you want and need to know first what the land itself wants. Reshad Feild's book *Here to Heal* describes this relationship to the land and the importance of cleaning up and creating order in the defined space. It is not widely understood that land is responsive to intent, but this is true. Conscious work, in the manner of Gurdjieff and the Fourth Way, consists of visualizing the completion of the work before starting and then filling up the time. Conscious work in the kitchen means focusing completely on what you are doing, with gratitude for the food that has given up its life to nourish yours, and also gratitude that you are able to do this work to serve (however you conceive of) the Divine through serving those who will eat the meal. If there is a kitchen group, they attune to each other before preparations begin. A meal so prepared has extraordinary flavor as well as nourishment. And any kind of work can be done with this same kind of focus and attunement. Try it and see how different a task seems.

As dowsers we are often asked to "look at" from a distance, with or without a map, the health of people or animals or the land and, if we receive all the permissions, to do what we can to help. The first thing we look at is the land and any buildings on it. We dowse to identify any positive earth energies such as energy leys, positive chi lines, domes, and water veins, but we also look for any negative water veins, negative chi lines, and any psychic or other damages that may be able to be healed through the divine beings and natural forces that respond to our prayers. Our role usually is simply to make requests.

Another approach to healing is the shamanic one. *Medicine for the Earth* by Sandra Ingerman gives her approach on how to transmute personal and environmental toxins. She suggests visualizations, ceremonies, and rituals to use while learning to do this work.

Central to both the dowsing and the shamanic understanding of this work are awareness of the interconnection of all that is and the power of Love.

The earth is much in need of all that any of us can do to help in the current ecological crisis that is so largely human-made and includes accelerating climate change, massive species extinctions, and increasing pollution—not only of the land but of the rivers and the oceans. (It is very disheartening to learn that even medical waste connected with the Covid-19 pandemic has been thrown away carelessly and is now being found in the sea.)

In *Spiritual Ecology: The Cry of the Earth* editor Llewellyn Vaughan-Lee has brought together many essays relating to the sacred nature of creation. I wish that this collection and Thomas Berry's *The Great Work: Our Way into the Future* could be read by everyone, for recognition of the sacredness of the earth is essential for human beings to understand all that needs to be changed.

Braiding Sweetgrass: Indigenous Wisdom, Scientific Knowledge and the Teaching of Plants by Robin Wall Kimmerer is another excellent book about restoring awareness of the sacred nature of the earth. As both a member of the Potawatomi Nation and an environmental biologist, the author's teaching is aimed at awakening in her students love for the land and its plants and creatures that give us everything that enables us to live. "The moral covenant of reciprocity calls us to honor our responsibilities for all we have been given, for all that we have taken."[3] But beyond that, it is really only deep love for the earth and her inhabitants that will make the difference in whether enough people care enough to make the major changes that will have to be made if human beings are going to be able to have a future on the earth.

7

Harmony with the Cosmos

IN THE definition of geomancy is the concept that human activity needs to be in harmony not only with the earth but with the cosmos. In connection with the cosmos this statement can have at least two meanings. First is an understanding of a hierarchy that comes down from the One, the Divine, the Totality, meaning that we understand our rightful place within that hierarchy not as "lords of all we survey" but as what some would understand as being God's servants and regents here on earth, with our role being that of responsible custodians, and, as Reshad Feild has said, "transformers of subtle energies." Second is harmony with the cosmic bodies that are also part of our universe.

In what we know of human history there always has been awareness of the sky. The sun and moon have been revered by many civilizations. Seyyed Hossein Nasr called the sun "the intelligible principle of the universe," as love certainly is. I think of Daniel Ladinsky's version of words by the Sufi Hafiz (c. 1320–1389):

> the sun never says to the earth,
>
> "You owe me."
>
> Look
> what happens
> with a love like that—
>
> it lights the whole
> world.[1]

The sun is what we first understand of light, and we are totally dependent on the sun for the photosynthesis that gives us vegetation—the trees and plants and grasses without which there would be a barren planet.

In *The Garden of Truth* Seyyed Hossein Nasr wrote, "it is also to pierce with the light of the intellect all veils of duality and otherness to return to the Sun of the Self, which is the origin of all selves and the source of the intellect shining within those who have realized the state of perfect servanthood."[2] The way of knowledge is central to this path, but always combined with love, faith, and correct action, as a light that returns the human being to its Source—the Supernal Sun. The symbol of the sun then has that surround of meaning always present to those following that path.

Saint Francis, beloved Christian saint who is also thought of by some as an exemplar of the Sufi tradition, spoke of Brother Sun:

> Be praised, my Lord, with all your creatures,
> Especially Lord Brother Sun,
> To whom we owe both day and light,
> For he is beautiful, radiant and of great splendor;
> Of you, most high, he is the emblem.[3]

The moon has also been revered, with many stories told about it. The phases of the moon give us calendrical markers, and we have learned that long ago ancestors had very precise understandings of such indicators.

Many have gardened by the phases of the moon, their wisdom passed down through notations, proverbs, folktales, and gardening books. The waxing moon is generally recommended for new growth and beginnings—the sowing of large areas (as of grain) and the sowing of leafy crops. Flowers are to be sown in the first quarter, berry bushes in the second quarter. In drought it is recommended to sow seeds as close as possible to the full moon. Grafting, taking cuttings, and picking fruits and vegetables for immediate consumption are best done during a waxing moon. The harvesting of herbs and of grapes for winemaking is best done as close to the full moon as possible.

The waning moon is best for sowing root vegetables and plants when a strong root system first needs to be developed. Trees and saplings and strawberries are best planted in the third quarter. Perennials are best divided and compost piles started in the waning moon, and crops are best harvested then for long-term storage. These are just some of the suggestions from *The Lunar Garden* by E. A. Crawford.

Rudolf Steiner developed biodynamic agriculture, very dependent on cycles of the moon. Maria Thun worked out further relationships of the moon with stars and constellations, and she has a very detailed annual biodynamic almanac. Also based on her work is the Stella Natura calendar, published by the Kimberton Hills community in Pennsylvania, also showing when to plant root vegetables, leafy vegetables, or those where the flower is the food or wanted product. Although these calendars may show just a time slot of a few hours for planting certain kinds of seeds on a given day, studies as well as individual reports indicate that superior crops are obtained by following the schedule.

An interesting account of the making of some biodynamic preparations appears in *Secrets of the Soil*. These may seem bizarre to the casual reader, such as packing manure into cow horns, burying these over the winter, and then using just a small amount of the odorless result stirred into water as fertilizer. Bizarre, yes, but the methods used are the result of ongoing and intensive study and care. The bottom line is that the preparations work, and so their use spreads quickly in areas where farmers see and judge by the results obtained.

Beyond the sun and the moon, there is also evidence that different planets affect different plant species. In *The Spirit of Trees* Fred Hageneder wrote of the finding that different tree species are linked with different planets. With the alignment of Earth and Moon and Mars, oak buds expand slightly. Beech responds to Saturn, elm to Mercury, ash to the Sun, and birch to Venus. It is interesting to think of correlations to tales and myths. Ash, for example, has traditionally been thought to be Yggdrasil, the world tree on which Odin hung for wisdom, with all that spins out from that association.

Keith Critchlow said that Alexander Thom felt that the pole star was vital for the orientation of northern British stone circles. It is at the end of the handle of what is known as the Little Dipper or Ursa Minor. The Big Dipper or Ursa Major is seen as circling around this pole star, and aligned, the two stars at the far end of this dipper point to this North Star, also called Polaris, that symbolizes in the Sufi tradition the vertical direction known as the "orient." The "occident" is all that is flat below, but north to the orient means up, a vertical energy toward what is conceived of in that tradition as the hierarchy and the world "above" our world.

Various other stars are associated with different areas of occult wisdom. Astrology is a complicated way of looking at the patterns and effects of celestial configurations on our lives. Of course there is an effect: everything that is, is connected. To become a master of the skill of reading such effects and patterns requires much time and effort. As with everything, there are always those who take shortcuts and set themselves up as more knowledgeable than they are. Even competent astrology is only one set of the multiple patterns that help to shape our lives.

In his introduction to *The Great Work: Our Way into the Future*, Thomas Berry wrote of our urgent need to learn how "to sustain the natural world so that the natural world can sustain us." Current science constantly surprises us with new discoveries about the always-greater-than-realized vastness and complexity of the universe, while it also becomes ever more clear that essential to our human survival is recognition of the sacredness of the entire cosmos and a different understanding of and treatment of our planet and all the other beings and kingdoms that share our earth home. The choices human beings have made for many years have caused great harm to the whole ecosystem, way beyond the current awareness of most people, and this must be understood and major and difficult changes made if there is to be a future for human beings, as well as for a great many other creatures and plants. The rate of extinction has risen drastically, much of it based on unwise human choices and actions.

And now we have a pandemic. "There is no hiding place down here." Everything is connected, and now people have to begin to understand that there are no walls or isolation policies that can separate us from the fact that the inhabitants of the earth are all in this together and to survive must learn to care about, help, and cooperate with each other. This means learning to appreciate that diversity in humankind is as important as it is in all the kingdoms, and also that learning about different spiritual paths may well bring surprise at what we share, and may deepen and enrich our understandings of our own traditions. Fear creates hate. Love is the Way.

8

The Mineral Kingdom and Mountains

IF YOU are interested in learning about the use of gemstones and crystals and their essences and elixirs in healing, *Vibrational Medicine* by Richard Gerber is a good starting place for investigating this field. I am influenced by cautions expressed by both Reshad Feild and by Oscar Morphis, MD, the expert radiation therapist who participated with Pir Vilayat in a weekend we attended on healing with light and sound. The cautions are about using crystals in healing without fully understanding their power and when and in what ways they should—and also very important, should not—be used.

However, if one is willing to spend the time to really study this subject, there are genuine therapeutic uses for gemstones and crystals, and for essences and elixirs made from them.

Energy of the mineral kingdom is not like our own; many consider the kingdom to be animate but with a different time frame from our own. Stones can "talk" and can hold impressions for a very long time. Those who believe that they have communicated with the stones at sacred sites affirm this.

In *The Secret Teachings of Plants* Stephen Harrod Buhner wrote of his experience of having been touched by a mountain being that seemed to awaken from millennia of contemplation to briefly notice tiny him. He described the power of its glance and that it was "old beyond knowing," with little to do with human beings.

Minerals do seem to feel. When driving where human beings have cut through stone ledges to create thruways, sometimes one can sense the pain of the severed stones.

The Mineral Kingdom and Mountains

In *Nature's Silent Music* Philip S. Callahan wrote of a weak repelling force, diamagnetism, and its opposite attractor, paramagnetism. Fertile soil from eroded volcanic rock, he says, is highly paramagnetic, while most organic substances are diamagnetic. Paramagnetism means the ability to collect or resonate with the magnetism of the earth and the sun. There are many theories of origin of the round towers of Ireland, scattered around the country in what appeared to Callahan to be a replica of a star map of the northern night sky at the December solstice. It seems that they were built before the Viking raids, although probably were used protectively during that time, for underground passages leading a distance away have been found. Callahan says that the towers are highly paramagnetic and so act as magnetic antennae, resonating with cosmic radio wavelengths and magnetic field energies, fertilizing the fields with cosmic energy. There are doorways high off the ground and at different levels, and the towers contain varying amounts of soil, each tower filled to a particular level to be receptive to the incoming frequency.

Granite is highly paramagnetic, and Callahan says that the early Celts understood the healing force in granite standing stones. He also says that rocks, stones, and even soil, if it contains sufficient volcanic eroded rock, are antenna collectors. Diamagnetic organic matter is also necessary; it stores water while paramagnetism controls the evaporation of water. He suggests the building of miniature round towers in gardens, as is described in *Secrets of the Soil* by Tompkins and Bird, adding volcanic gravel or ash to organic earth to make the soil resonant with the sun.

The concept of the holiness of mountains is part of many cultures. Feng shui and other traditions understand powerful earth currents to emanate from and to travel to other mountains.

Edwin Bernbaum in the November 1988 "The Mountain" issue of *Parabola* says that many cultures think of a mountain as the source of life and water, as a center—an axis linking heaven, earth, and hell, and as a conduit to this world for energies both divine and demonic. Some cultures view the capital of a country as a mountain centered in the ruler's realm on which he sits, drawing on the power of the deity of that place and often perceived as reincarnating that deity. Sometimes the height of mountains makes them thought of as realms of light and bliss. Mount Athos in Greece is thought of as an earthly paradise by the monks living there. Shiva is thought to sit on Mount Kailas. The summit of Mount Fuji, Bernbaum says, is viewed by the Japanese as the mandala of the Buddha. Mountains have been places for sacrifice and shrines for veneration. Croagh Patrick in Ireland is a place of pilgrimage, as are many mountains around the world. Ayer's Rock in Australia is considered sacred as part of the dreamtime of the ancestors. The San Francisco Peaks of Arizona are seen by the Hopis as a kiva housing ancestral spirits and kachinas.

W. Y. Evans-Wentz, the Celtic and Buddhist scholar, finished his earth life in California, where in his final book, *Cuchama and Sacred Mountains*, he explored parallels between the spiritual teachings of native peoples there and Hindus and Tibetans. Evans-Wentz hoped for a cultural rebirth that would unify the psychic traditions of East and West. He thought that the "shining beings" of the Native Americans were what were known to the Celts as fairies and to the Hindus as devas.

In myth one of the most persistent images is that of Shambhala, which means in Sanskrit a place of peace and tranquility. James Hilton's novel *Lost Horizon*, about what he called Shangri-La, and the movie made from it, tell of a secret place where wisdom and beauty will be protected during the difficult coming times. This sanctuary within the mountains of Asia cannot be found by looking for it, and once there, people are not supposed to leave.

The Mineral Kingdom and Mountains

The Shambhala vision of Chogyam Trungpa in *Shambhala: The Sacred Path of the Warrior* includes the idea that the key to warriorship and the first principle of the Shambhala vision is not being afraid of who you are, which in that tradition is the definition of bravery. Heroism and kindness are combined, with the thought that we must do what we can to help the world.

Victoria LePage's book *Shambhala* is an excellent overview of this tradition. Some think that the initial impulse for Shambhala came from as far back as Cro-Magnon man. When the world axis was aligned with the magnetic and north poles, Hyperborea—sharing many of the qualities attributed to Shambhala—was thought to be at the back of the north wind, where Apollo went for three months of the year. In the first millennium Scythians told of a place like Shambhala in the far north, so an early location for this idea seems to have been associated with the pole.

Perhaps 25,000 years ago thought of this center seems to have shifted to Asia, where different peoples locate it in slightly different areas. Some scholars think it was a sister city to Atlantis. Mount Meru and Mount Kailas have been suggested as the site, as have been the Hindu Kush, the Altai Mountains, and the area around Balkh (where Rumi was born) in Afghanistan.

In the nineteenth century a Russian Christian sect knew it as Belovodye, "white waters," a lost valley best known throughout Asia as Shambhala. The Hyperboreans called their site white island, but thought of it as near the Arctic Circle. Mount Meru means "white mountain."

The King of Shambhala is said to be the true king of the world, in direct touch with God. The Buddha is supposed to have taught the Kalachakra tradition. Some say it is far older, but this is supposed to be the central teaching of Shambhala, related to kundalini and breath, with much of the teaching secret.

The Mineral Kingdom and Mountains

Tibetan guidebooks give directions, starting with familiar territory but becoming mythic. You can't go to Shambhala unless you are ready and it is allowed. The sacred call Kalagiya! indicates that the way is open.

In *The Way to Shambhala*, Edwin Bernbaum tells how Shambhala is often pictured in mandala form, as an eight-petalled lotus, with the kingship in the center and two rings of surrounding mountains. This lotus shape corresponds to the nerves of the heart center, and this pattern symbolizes this most important center of the psychic nervous system where the highest mind, the one capable of knowing the true nature of reality, is hidden.

There are thoughts that Shambhala is invisible until a certain state of consciousness is reached that allows it to be seen. Some lamas think it is in this world, some in another dimension or even on another planet. In *Entering the Circle* Olga Kharitidi, MD, is told that the beings living there are another branch of humanity.

In Shambhala they have understandings of matter and mind superior to our own. The Nazis were interested and sent several expeditions to Tibet to search, but not surprisingly, these failed.

Nicholas Roerich tried in an expedition to return a piece of meteorite stone to Shambhala. This was part of the larger Chintamani stone that was said to give telepathic inner guidance and to transform the consciousness of those in contact with it. LePage wrote that the black stone at the Ka'aba at Mecca and that of the shrine of Cybele are believed by some occultists to be part of the same meteorite that is alleged to have come from the Orion constellation, probably from Sirius.

The search for the Holy Grail is thought by some to relate to Shambhala. In Wolfram von Eschenbach's *Parzival* the grail is a stone. The philosophers' stone of the alchemists is perhaps related to this as well. Some authors think that all esoteric traditions of the world are related to Shambhala, as well as all journeys, including those in the *Odyssey*, *The Conference of the Birds*, and the *Divine Comedy*.

The books I've read have commented on the totally ecumenical nature of Shambhala. Some think this kingdom may be too large to see, spread over many countries, with individuals working for the betterment of the world. The Masters of Wisdom, the Khwajagan, may have some connection with this tradition. According to J. G. Bennett, they were known for respecting all traditions, feeling that something good could be learned from each of them and not disputing or having rivalries.

In his books about the Sufi tradition, Henry Corbin wrote about Hurqalya, the eighth clime, reached by the emerald rock at the top of Mount Qaf. The mystic pole is this mountain and it is right under the polestar. One goes to Hurqalya after death but can go there now, and beings from there can come here, as in *Entering the Circle* the shaman can go to "Belovodia" and return.

In Peter Gold's *Navajo and Tibetan Sacred Wisdom: The Circle of the Spirit* Shambhala is shown as the model of the Tibetan sacred world's enlightened civilization. Its armies are someday to vanquish human ignorance and purify the world of obstacles to compassion and enlightenment.

Shambhala is an enduring symbol of a heaven on earth to which many would like to find entrance. It represents the lost paradise where all things are "well again" and we are in harmony with nature. In some spiritual traditions it is in consciousness where we may find what we seek and through which we may become able to be in that special world at the same time that we are living in this one.

9

The World of Plants

THE SECRET Life of Plants by Peter Tompkins and Christopher Bird, published in 1973, described studies by Cleve Backster and Marcel Vogel that show that plants have consciousness and are aware of human intent regarding them. Pam Montgomery in *Plant Spirit Healing*, published in 2008, mentioned that a new field of plant neurobiology has emerged, with a first symposium in May 2005 in Florence, Italy. Plants are now more widely understood as able to process information and to communicate.

The ideas of a green thumb and of talking to plants have seeped into popular consciousness, but some individuals have done this in a very wholehearted way, among these the agricultural chemist George Washington Carver, who turned the sweet potato and the peanut into hundreds of separate products, and who said that he talked to plants and through loving them called forth from them their best. "All flowers talk to me and so do hundreds of little living things in the woods. I learn what I know by watching and loving everything."[1] Although Carver created fortunes for thousands, he seldom took out patents on his ideas, saying "God did not charge me or you for making peanuts. Why should I profit from their products?"[2]

The Findhorn garden in Scotland is well known for exceptional plant growth in an inhospitable spot. Participants feel, as Dorothy Maclean and others have reported, that this is the result of communication between people and the invisible-to-most nature intelligences that they credit with "overlooking" plant growth and instructing them about the wishes and needs of particular plant groups. The name they give these intelligences is devas, and they understand each of these to represent a plant group consciousness, but there are other nature intelligences that also have specific jobs.

Roc Ogilvie at Findhorn found that he could see and communicate with a faun, a nature spirit, and later with the great god Pan, who told Roc that he was "the servant of Almighty God, and I and my subjects are willing to come to the aid of mankind, in spite of the way he has treated us and abused nature, if he affirms belief in us and asks for our help."[3] Roc wrote, "Pan is a universal energy, a cosmic energy, which is constantly found throughout the whole of nature. He could appear personified in many different places at the same time and should never be thought of as restricted to a corner of the garden or sitting on a hilltop beside a gorse bush."[4] Later he added, "Rather than using force to bring about changes in plants, it would be much better if man would ask the nature spirits to bring them about by modifying the etheric counterpart."[5] This is reminiscent of the idea that disease manifests first in the etheric body, where, if noticed, it can be treated (also in a subtle way) before it manifests physically.

In *Secrets from the Lives of Trees* there is an interview with Marcel Vogel, who, when he went to Findhorn, wanted to meet Roc. Nobody had seen Roc for a long time, but there in Vogel's room was Roc, waiting for him after telepathically picking up his wish. The next day they went and sat by a bush to experience the nonmaterial nature spirits. There were no phenomena except for the movement of air, but for Vogel it was a profound experience. Form, he felt, is only a construction the nature spirits offer in order to communicate. When Vogel projected thoughts of love and well-being to the bush, he saw the whole bush shimmer and shake.

Machaelle Small Wright has described achieving the same sort of working relationship as at Findhorn with nature intelligences in her Perelandra garden in Virginia. Part of the agreement in both places is keeping a separate space, into which people do not go, that is reserved wild for the nature intelligences. This seems to me to be similar to the spaces reserved for the kami spirits recognized in the Shinto religion in gardens in Japan.

Many medicines in the current allopathic repertoire are chemical imitations of plant substances. But the same argument holds as against synthetic rather than natural fertilizers: chemical formulas leave out perhaps the most important aspect of what its formulators have been attempting to copy: life force is more than a chemical formula. Also, because we often combine what in nature is not combined, a problem of disposal is created for which nature is not prepared and the ramifications of which cannot be predicted. This disposal problem includes allopathic medicines excreted or put into water systems through toilets as well as those disposed of through landfills or burning. I am grateful to Stephen Harrod Buhner for pointing this out in *The Lost Language of Plants*. TV news reports are that prescription drug residues are being found in drinking water in major cities across the United States.

Buhner also mentioned some extremely disturbing findings that the spread of pathogenic bacteria, strengthened because of too widespread use of farm antibiotics, seems to occur without direct contact. Have morphic or morphogenetic fields that spread this harm been created by widespread antibiotic use? Everything is connected. We cannot think anymore of discrete events.

It is thought that we have discovered only a small fraction of the plants and animals that share our planet. Edward O. Wilson in *The Diversity of Life* estimated with others that there are 1.4 million known species of organisms, although he said that evolutionary biologists feel that this is probably less than a tenth of those living on the earth. This makes all the more serious accelerating losses and extinctions through pollution, through clear-cutting, through climate change, and through all the other harms that we as a species are continuing more and more rapidly to inflict upon the world. We are aware of some losses but are undoubtedly totally unaware of many more. Elizabeth Kolbert, author of *The Sixth Extinction: An Unnatural History*, published in 2014, feels that if we continue at the same pace there will be loss of 75 percent of all species on earth within a few hundred years.

In *Plant Intelligence and the Imaginal Realm* Buhner wrote about the crisis about to occur in allopathic medicine as drug-resistant bacteria proliferate, for realization is growing that bacteria can grow much faster than had been understood. He wrote *Herbal Antibiotics* and *Herbal Antivirals* with his suggestions for natural alternatives and natural remedies—herbal medicines. He has written many helpful books, including several related to Lyme disease, and also the foreword to Timothy Lee Scott's *Invasive Plant Medicine*, which is about the ecological benefits and healing abilities of a number of what are considered to be invasive plants, plants that are now mistakenly being eradicated as not native, although it seems that they have come here as part of Gaia's intelligence. Japanese knotweed, for example, can be used in the treatment of Lyme disease and tends to move into infected areas before the disease is discovered there. Buhner says that it also helps the body to process numbers of toxins and cancers.

Mellie Uyldert, a Dutch writer, in the 1980 English edition of *The Psychic Garden*, noted that plants that are remedies for illness come into manifestation where there is need. Pam Montgomery also says that many herbalists have realized this. In *The Psychic Garden* Uyldert described how, in a retirement community in Holland with a number of cancer patients, marigolds (what we call pot marigolds or calendulas) suddenly appeared and reappeared again and again for several years until the last of the cancer patients had died. When these marigolds were no longer needed, they went out of manifestation and did not return. These marigolds, she wrote, were a cure for cancer, although this was not recognized by the people they came to help.

Herbal medicine, where parts of plants are used as medicines, has a very long history, including a contemporary one. Rosemary Gladstar, Susun Weed, Diane Stein, and Stephen Harrod Buhner are among those who teach contemporary uses of herbal medicines. But there are also other subtle understandings of plant use.

After time spent in India, Edward Bach, a British doctor, began to think of the essences of plants as possibly healing. He discovered his flower remedies by experiment and intuitive recognition of what specific flowers could do. His discoveries have helped countless people with essences that assist in transforming emotional states that could otherwise result in disease. The essences are made in most cases by putting flower petals into spring water in sunlight and then bottling this mother essence, with some brandy as a preservative. Two drops of this mixture in water is a usual dose, except that for Rescue Remedy four drops are used, so that very little substance is involved: this is an "energy" medicine. The Bach Rescue Remedy, made up of six essences, is something that we keep with us at all times for emergency and high stress situations for people, animals, birds, and plants. There are many books about Bach flower essences, including some relatively recent ones showing uses by topical application to body zones charted for specific remedies.

Since the time of Edward Bach there has been a proliferation of interest in flower essences, and a vast quantity of them are now made in many parts of the world from local plant

The World of Plants

materials, each to help with specific emotional and sometimes physical states. Some of these uses of flower essences are described in *Vibrational Medicine* by Richard Gerber and *Flower Essences* by Gurudas. Some practitioners feel that local plants have the most powerful effects; this corresponds to the localvore idea of eating what is grown in the area where you live.

The idea of plant spirit medicine has been spread by Eliot Cowan and others. Beginning with using homeopathic preparations made from plants, Cowan says in *Plant Spirit Medicine* that he moved to most often using drops of filaree flower essence, requesting that this as messenger summon a particular plant spirit. Diagnosis or treatment of an illness is not part of it, he reminds readers. "There is only one active ingredient in plant medicines—friendship. A plant spirit heals a patient as a favor to its friend-in-dreaming." Cowan says that "In all cultures there exist individuals who have especially vivid experiences with the spirits of nature. These are the shamans. Shamans make friends of the spirits of nature and call upon them for help with everyday affairs."[6]

In the shamanic tradition a typical way of relating to another kingdom—in this case the plant kingdom—would be "journeying" to the plant spirit to ask for help. In my own dowsing paradigm it now feels right just to ask, when this is appropriate and when I have received the permissions, that my request for specific plant spirit help be heard.

When I mention "permissions," this is what I mean. First, we must be asked for help by the individual involved or, if that is not possible, then by someone very close to that individual, or we must have received permission from that individual. Next we dowse—and to do this one must have become a competent dowser, asking the Highest and Best that we know (however we conceive of that) three questions: May I? (Do I have permission from the Source?) Can I? (Do

I have the skill, especially at this time?) Should I? (Am I the one to do this, and is this the time to do it?). I usually add a fourth query: Is this the truth? If we don't get yes responses to all these queries, we do not proceed, even when dowsing for ourselves or family members. And this is what we always teach when we teach dowsing. This is very important when we are asked to dowse for someone else and especially if we are going to request any changes. We do not want to cause any harm, however inadvertently, and we cannot know the ramifications of all situations without this direction from a Higher Source.

If it is the singing of songbirds in the early morning that is nature's way of opening the stomata of plants to receive nutrients, few people are aware of this finding. In many places songbirds have been hunted for food or feathers. There is terrible history in our own country of mindless "sport" in shooting whole flocks of birds. When climate changes, clear-cutting, pollution, and depredations by marauding house cats are increasingly threatening declining songbird populations, more attention to this finding is needed.

Nature can produce out of seemingly nothing, out of the "silence"—what David Bohm might call the implicate order—what is needed if attention is there. Stephen Harrod Buhner confirms this idea in his foreword to Pam Montgomery's *Plant Spirit Healing*, where he says that plants can sense a chemical needed by an ecosystem and manufacture it—a reminder of the power of the invisible and of the active consciousness of plants.

Peter Wohlleben's *The Hidden Life of Trees* describes how trees relate as do human families and communicate, share nutrients, and warn each other of impending dangers.

Flowers have been the subject of myths and legends all over the world. Books on Victorian flower meanings have been popular, with many correspondences appearing to have had their origin in ancient Persian understandings. Gretchen Scoble and Ann Field in *The Meaning of Flowers* wrote that by the end of the Romantic period in the West flowers had become a secret code. The leaves on a branch might indicate time and date of a rendezvous, the blooms the intent of the meeting. From these secret codes the Victorian "Language of Flowers" was created, sometimes with different meanings for flowers in different versions. Flower code books were published, and coded bouquets, giving messages through the flowers chosen, were very popular.

Flowers, plants, and trees have been understood as symbols and as such have appeared in art and in gardens, where sight of them was intended to evoke associations to which we today are mostly blind. There will be more about this in the section on gardens.

William Irwin Thompson was intrigued by the tale in which Rapunzel, imprisoned in a tower, lets down her braids to allow the king's son to climb up to her. A wicked sorceress cuts the braids and the prince falls into thorns that blind him. Later he finds Rapunzel and her tears falling on his eyes cause him to see again, and they live long and happily afterwards. In *Imaginary Landscape: Making Worlds of Myth and Science*, Thompson described how he found in the plant Rapunzel many elements of the story (such as braids and tower). He wrote many pages on meanings and implications of the story, including realization that the plant itself is the tale. How does this happen? It seems that much in the world is encoded, waiting for us to notice.

In *The Spirit of Trees* Fred Hageneder quoted Viktor Schauberger's 1930 comment, "Without the forest, no water; without water, no bread; without bread, no life."[7]

Hageneder pointed out the drastic decrease in the earth's magnetic field that parallels deforestation: "With the clear felling of woodlands Man is bringing about the decline of the

Earth's magnetic field which, with the magnetosphere, creates the planet's only effective protective shield against hard particle radiation from the Sun and the cosmos."[8]

We read the Francis Thompson line, "Thou canst not stir a flower without the troubling of a star." The reverse seems to be true as well. Hageneder reported that radiation from supernovas influences tree growth. An 807-year-old juniper in Tajikistan, on the upper tree line, was shown to have significant slowing of growth for the fifteen years following supernova events. "Every star that dies in our galaxy is therefore perceived by trees."[9] Everything is connected.

Leaf buds, Hagenender wrote, show a fortnightly rhythm at the alignment of the earth and moon with a third celestial body specific to that particular plant species.

Theodor Schwenk wrote that on a summer's day 3,500 gallons of water are drawn through an acre of woodland into the atmosphere. This is only one of the gifts of trees, for they give us and other creatures shade for comfort and shade for watercourses that is necessary for good water quality. Trees provide beauty and absorb chlorofluorocarbons that destroy the ozone layer, remove particulates and gases including carbon dioxide (an acre of trees is estimated to remove approximately thirteen tons of dust and gases in a year). Trees fertilize the land, are windbreaks, and their roots hold unstable banks in place. At the University of Colorado it was found that 47,000 aspen trees arose from the root of a single tree, thus becoming the largest, heaviest organism known in the world. We know the importance of trees in the air we breathe, and they provide food: fruit, nuts, and syrup from sap. Many medicines come from trees, or trees were the prototypes from which medicines were derived (such as aspirin from the willow), and trees provide homeopathic remedies and flower essences as well as plant spirit medicine. They are home to many creatures and provide rubber and heating fuel and materials for construction of homes and other buildings, fences, boats, and furniture. There would be a very different and sorry world without trees.

Many traditions hold trees as sacred or consider them as elder statesmen. Within groves in parts of Japan at least one tree is considered to be sacred and home of the kami spirits. These trees are either protected by an enclosure or have a rope around them with thin strips of cloth attached to indicate that this is sacred space.

In his essay in *The Language of the Birds* William R. LaFleur referred to the question of whether the Bodhi tree was an inert part of the Buddha's enlightenment or was a companion without whom perfection could not have occurred. He mentioned also that in Buddhist literature there was for a long time controversy about whether or not plant life and trees were or were not sentient beings, although this seems to have been finally decided by saying that it could not be said that they were not. In Noh plays in Japan plants speak and act and help people to find the Way.

In folklore and myth the World Tree is of great importance, thought to be on the omphalos or at the axis mundi, the center of the world, often related to the polestar. It is on this tree named Yggdrasil that, after sacrificing an eye, Odin hung to receive his enlightenment. It is also the pole the shaman climbs, with his drum as his horse. It is the symbolic pole of the sun dance, the maypole, and the Christian cross. Roger Cook in his foreword to *The Tree of Life: Image for the Cosmos* wrote, "The trunk of the World Tree is the central pivot on which the world turns; a tree sacrifice is the way in which a god . . . is united with his transcendent, immortal self; and the structure of the tree is the pattern of ascent for contemplatives in many traditions."[10] A smaller version of this tree is often found beside a holy well. In Ireland this is often a hazel tree, frequently covered with strips of cloth signifying prayers.

Nasr reminded us that trees express the multiple states of being. They exist in this middle-earth world, but they also have great root systems below ground to the underworld, sometimes going down as deeply as the crowns of the trees rise into the heavens.

And there are all the additional folklore associations of trees. A rowan (mountain ash) planted near the house will keep witches away and animals from harm. Oak suggests Jupiter or Zeus and reminds us of the oak groves of the Druids. Willow has to do with female and lunar rhythms of life, with Brigit—the Celtic goddess—and protection against damp diseases. The apple tree is always in bloom in the Otherworld.

Celtic Tree Mysteries by Steve Blamires contains a great deal of information about the meaning of trees as related to Celtic tree ogham. His view is not that of the calendar of trees as described by Robert Graves in *The White Goddess*; he felt instead that the pre-Christian Celts were interested in the present and dated events by the Great Year that was approximately nineteen solar years, making a full cycle of sun, moon, and earth. Beithe, Luis, Nion, the way the ogham tree alphabet is often named, may refer to the Celtic god BeLiNos or to BeaLaN, meaning mouthful, which suggests ogham to have been an oral tradition, as he thinks it originally was, although we usually think of ogham as the marks made against a straight line, which we understand as indicating different letters.

Blamires said that the emphasis on their magical aspect without first knowing the physical properties of trees is not good; he mentioned the role of trees as "creators and filters of the atmosphere of the planet, something which is truly magical and upon which every other life form on Earth depends."[11] For Celtic tree magic he says that the main source of knowledge is Irish Celtic legends where specific trees are mentioned. The naming of the trees in these stories is deliberate, and, "if you keep in mind the magical meanings, uses, and symbolism of the trees, you will realize just how much information these ancient legends convey."[12]

One example is in *The Frenzy of Sweeney* (*Buile Suibhne Geilt*, translated by the Irish Text Society), although a modern version that more may now know is *Sweeney Astray* by Seamus Heaney. Blamires understands the tree poem in this story to be about the training of a shaman, his period of "visiting and searching" lasting a year, giving him his ability to communicate with the Green World. He completes his year of studying tree ogham and then has to go through a period of balancing, aided by trees and plants. Briar helps him clear away what is no longer needed, assisted by blackthorn that represents the Otherworld and movement between the two worlds. When threatened, Suibhne always takes refuge in the yew tree, symbolizing the pinnacle of achievement of one who knows all there is to know of tree ogham. The longest poem in the story starts with the oak, which represents the High King and Sovereignty of the Land, also Lord of the Hunt, which Suibhne has also become; the oak has an association with the planet Mars. The next tree, hazel, represents the death of the old self to clear the way for the new. The alder is the shield of the warrior, who has gained the protection of the trees. The blackthorn represents the need to "die before death." The flowing watercress lets Suibhne know that all will be well. The apple comforts and is the key to the Otherworld. He can now travel between the worlds. The rowan symbolizes magical powers. The thorn bush represents trials still to come. Then come the yew and the ivy—the yew the pinnacle of success, and the ivy representing the power and knowledge of all the trees. However, the ivy warns Suibhne not to become smug or it will bind him and keep him from progressing. The holly offers further trials but also protection if these trials are faced. The ash means progress through positive action. Birch means self-sacrifice and pushing farther and higher. The aspen represents acceptance of his achievements. The last tree, the oak, completes the circle but now at a higher level. One can stay or go on to another round of tests. Blamires feels that what many would view just as an affectionate poem about trees actually tells the story of trees training the shaman.

There are many other books available on tree meanings, including *The Celtic Tree Oracle* by Liz and Colin Murray, *Tree Wisdom* by Jacqueline Memory Paterson, *The Magic Garden* by Anthony S. Mercatante, and *The Folklore of Trees and Shrubs* by Laura C. Martin. Studying tree meanings can add a great deal to our appreciation of this kingdom.

In the Sufi tradition the palm tree is on the margin with the imaginal world and indicates a place of transition between this world and the world of the celestial earth. This does not mean imaginary world, but a world that exists beyond this world and that can be accessed through what Henry Corbin, in writing about Ibn 'Arabi, called the creative imagination. In Persian pictures, if you see the palm tree and there are no people in the picture, you are about to enter this imaginal world of Hurqalya, and you populate it yourself with your visionary body.

The cypress seen in such pictures represents immortality and what is "real," and that is why many representations of the tree of life in that part of the world are the cypress.

After all these dimensions to our thinking about trees, we turn now to how we treat trees in our society. It is certainly rarely with respect. To most, trees are a commodity, a resource, but, fortunately, not everyone feels this way.

The dying of the trees in recent times has been of great concern to some, among them Christopher Bird, who wrote and spoke about this often. Some things have been done to try to lessen the acidity of the rain that even here in Vermont has been sadly felt in the maple groves, but the threat persists.

The World of Plants

In an article in the *New Yorker* (February 25, 2008) Michael Specter says that an estimate of the huge footprints caused by the destruction of the rain forests in Brazil and Indonesia in the next twenty-four hours would be the same as if eight million people boarded airplanes at Heathrow and flew to New York. The destruction happening to the rain forests in Brazil recently is even more dismaying. The point is that stopping deforestation would be a major step toward slowing global warming.

We need to value our trees and to teach their importance and of course to do all that we can to make smaller our own carbon footprints. Also we need to be creative in what we can do to help the trees. Tree planting is encouraged by many groups, inspired by the story of Johnny Appleseed and the work of Richard St. Barbe Baker. Julia "Butterfly" Hill camped out for a long time in the crown of an ancient redwood, hoping thus to have its life spared and attention brought to the cutting of such giant trees. I have a card showing women of the Chipko ("to hug") movement in India in 1973 surrounding trees to save them from cutting.

The author Jan de Hartog used to go out with his dowsing rods and ask if there was a tree that needed his help, and he would be led to one that did: sometimes this meant just something as simple as removing a branch of another tree that had fallen on the one asking for help.

In Jean Giono's novel *The Man Who Planted Trees* the shepherd hero collects acorns and plants them and then sets out the young trees in a war-devastated area. After many years the trees have grown and restored the earth, even bringing back the springs that had dried up when the previous trees were destroyed.

Trees, those great and wise beings, are essential to life, so that gratitude is the appropriate human response to and for them, although one that is seldom expressed. Some who work with trees with respect have learned to ask permission of the trees before any cutting that has to be done and, if possible, do any cutting during the waning moon. Clear-cutting is never appropriate and has been described as comparable to book burning.

The idea of forest "management" seems on reflection to be arrogant. A forest is part of the Gaian system that is complex in ways beyond our human capacity to comprehend, as Lynn Margulis pointed out in her essay in *Talking on the Water*. In *The Sacred Balance* David Suzuki said,

> We are a long way from being able to make even an educated guess as to how to manage natural systems, especially ones as complex as forests, wetlands, prairies, oceans or the atmosphere. The Nobel laureate Richard Feynman once observed that trying to understand nature through science is like trying to figure out the rules of chess as you watch a game being played—but you can only see two squares at a time.[13]

We can learn to communicate with trees as with any life form. In *Sacred Trees* Nathaniel Altman quoted Walking Buffalo of the Storey tribe, who said that trees will talk to you if you listen and that he had learned a lot from them about weather, animals, and the Great Spirit.

10

The World of Animals

FOR MOST of us, pets have been the entrance to awareness of the animal kingdom. My husband and I were blessed in having the companionship first of two wonderful collies and then later some special shelties. Three of the shelties were littermates, but very different from each other. Rowan, the largest, lived for a little over eleven years, Liam for over fifteen years, and Molly, the mid-sized one, just over sixteen years. (If you are interested in learning more about their lives, *Going to the Dogs*, written by my husband, has been published by Finn Cara Press.) From the beginning the three dogs were a pack, with my husband as pack master. It was very interesting to watch the dynamics of a pack, but I had hoped to learn from these shelties something more of the invisible world, as I was able to do from our collie Brigit. Toward the end of his life Liam honored my wish and began to teach me. As did Brigit, he showed me when invisible presences came to call, coming to get my attention and waiting until I took out my pendulum to dowse who was here. Sometimes I quickly intuited who it was; at other times I'd have to ask "twenty questions": Is it —? Yes/no, and so on. All of these deceased dogs—the two collies and the three shelties—continued to visit here from time to time, but they were here most of the time in the months just before my husband's death. We didn't in any way try to bind their spirits here, but have always reassured them of our love that continues into their afterlife existence, and they know that they will always be welcome whenever it is "to the highest good" for them to visit here.

The World of Animals

They don't come as often now that my husband is with them in the spirit world, where someday I hope to join them. We know that our dear ones do go on after death, which is not the end, but rather the portal to the next step in the journey.

You will have noticed that I feel very matter-of-fact about the presence of what some would call ghosts. These are benign presences that have come to check on us, lend support, or to give us a message, and they are in no way harmful. Some discarnate entities, however, are harmful to the health of people or animals, and when they appear uninvited we do request, with permission, that they be escorted on to their next proper place of development. You can read more about this in *The Divining Heart*. This is not exorcism as that is usually understood. Most discarnate entities are not evil, but are usually beings that have not gone on as is appropriate and who, still clinging to the earth plane after their deaths, may sap the energy of living human beings or animals. It is a kindness to those beings to ask that they be helped to go on to where they are meant to be.

A later dog friend, an older sheltie named Finn Cara, came to us from owners who loved but could no longer keep him. Finn was a dear and gracious companion, and we enjoyed noting how he had been instructed about his life here by our spirit dogs. I was very grateful for his presence, especially during the seven years he was with me here after my husband's death, as Dick had requested him to be.

Animal communication is a growing interest, and there are a number of worthy communicators and books. Some of our favorite communication books are those by Amelia Kinkade and Penelope Smith. As Rupert Sheldrake's writing about angels within a scientific context adds a whole new dimension to angelology, in *The Language of Miracles* Amelia Kinkade does something similar for animal communication.

The foreword to her book is by Bernie S. Siegel, MD, an initial skeptic she helped to find a missing pet. Throughout the book the language and rationale of what Kinkade teaches is based on her understanding of new physics. What emerges from the book is a picture of animal intelligence and foresight in some cases far superior to those of human beings, and more accepting and more loving as well. I think of J. Allen Boone writing in *Kinship with All Life* about the German shepherd Strongheart, who always accurately evaluated each new person he met, far more astutely than Boone himself was able to do.

Realization of the (at least) equality and sometimes superiority of many animals to human beings comes through these writings and is recognized as true by those of us who have had close relationships with other species. For information about Strongheart, Boone was taught to go directly to Strongheart and not to various so-called experts on dogs. We learned to do this with our own dogs.

How I have done this is to sit quietly in order to focus, ask the permissions, and then request contact with the individual with whom I want to talk. I then ask my questions in a binary (yes/no) format and dowse the answers. Having dowsed now for many years, questions come quickly into my mind and often I "know" or receive the answers even before I use my pendulum, although I do use it then to double-check. I also often asked my husband to check to see if he agreed with what I had dowsed or if he could add anything to the query and response. What I found is that not only do the dogs know a great deal about things related to themselves, but they know a great deal about others as well—both animals and people, both nearby and far away. And, to my surprise, they know this not in the limited way human beings have usually thought of dog intelligence. This would to my mind corroborate both Kinkade's and Boone's findings and perhaps go beyond, and this has been an unexpected gift of the ongoing relationship with the dogs in their spirit form. As an example, Liam told me something that I had not thought of—that to prevent headaches when viewing TV or DVDs my husband needed glasses made for the exact distance from where he usually sat to the television screen; we followed Liam's advice and he was right. I am only sorry that I did not realize this wider possibility of communication long before I did.

Learning to communicate also allows us to understand at least a little of what another being's world is like. The more I learn, the more I am sure that the world of each species is quite different from ours and from those of other species, and that each kingdom has skills and senses that other kingdoms do not have and that we can only begin to imagine.

In *The Secret Language of Life* Brian J. Ford says,

> Our vision of reality derives from the interplay of the human senses. Many other forms of sense in the living world are not possessed by humankind, and other organisms can detect things in ways that we cannot imagine. Some can sense the earth's magnetism, watch the changes of polarised light, see heat rays in the dark, or create an image out of ultrasound. Sea creatures construct detailed pictures of their surroundings through pressure waves in the oceans, or find their hidden prey through electrical currents in the water. Insects do daily problem-solving. Plants turn in the dark, ready to face the morning sun. Tribes of creatures great and small are bonded by their emotions, and use languages of subtle complexity.[1]

Ford says that the "richness of sensation in other forms of life" has been overlooked. A falling tree in the forest is detected by innumerable organisms. "Some species use star maps to guide their nocturnal activities."[2] His book is a strong beginning toward understanding some of the many ways in which animals and plants feel and communicate.

In *The Pig Who Sang to the Moon* Jeffrey Moussaieff Masson wrote about the emotional life of farm animals. His caring account calls for reassessment of how animals raised for food typically are considered and treated and makes a strong case for adopting a vegetarian or vegan lifestyle.

All the kingdoms are worthy of respect and have much to teach us. Human beings are not the top of the pyramid, but only part of the group that all together make up the Divine Symphony. Our human arrogance stands in the way of learning: humility is a much more appropriate attitude.

It is so heartening to be able to expand our relationship with our dear family members (often called pets), but what a boon being able to communicate with them would be to those in the veterinary services—and what a boon to those who bring their dear ones to the vet for help. In an emergency or with a frail animal, how wonderful also to know the results of what lab tests or sometimes painful procedures would be without having to inflict them on a patient, which is what learning to dowse potentially has to offer.

In the Sufi tradition the word "dog" is sometimes used as an analog for "heart," which is in contrast to the way dogs are sometimes treated in Eastern cultures and sadly even sometimes in our own. Dog lovers know that many dogs have exceptional heart and healing qualities. Specially trained dogs are now welcomed into hospitals and nursing homes, where their presence brings comfort and sometimes more to those they visit. And caregiver dogs allow many disabled people to live fuller lives.

Trisha Pope, a sound healer from Quebec, told us of her own dog, Pooka, who accompanied Trisha to her Montreal office where she saw patients, and who "told" an animal communicator that healing was also her work, especially that she was a "crying specialist" and knew the different kinds of crying and how to comfort and support the cryer. After hearing this, Trisha realized that this was so and that they were a team, and she complimented Pooka frequently on her work. Once when Trisha was lying down at home with a severe headache, Pooka came beside her and stayed for a time with her paw on Trisha's head. Then she would lick Trisha's face and put her paw back on her forehead. Trisha said that after a time of this her headache had almost gone.

Often when we think of a human/animal interaction we think of Saint Francis and how he tamed the wolf of Gubbio and had birds and animals flock around him. Few know that this is not the only spiritual tradition to have reported that kind of interaction. For example, as Idries Shah described in *The Sufis*, similar stories were told of Najmuddin Kubra, who lived sixty years before Saint Francis. And *Beasts and Saints*, the translations by Helen Waddell of tales dating mostly from the fourth through seventh centuries, includes stories of Egyptian Desert Fathers and Celtic saints who also interacted with creatures.

In the shamanic tradition there has always been a very strong connection between the shaman and the creatures that guide and help the shaman. Sometimes there is a creature that speaks so that the shaman can understand, or it may be a sign from the creature that directs the shaman.

In his introduction to *The Language of the Birds*, David M. Guss says that the shaman's journey is a linguistic one, for the shaman enters a trance through words and receives the message sought in another language, "the secret esoteric one that spirits and animals use in their own world. This is . . . the one that Shamans speak to one another, and refer to as 'the Language of the Birds.'"[3]

Native American traditions pay much attention to signs. The meaning of a particular bird flight, the appearance of a particular animal at a specific time—all such signs are considered to be part of the universe's answers to questions being asked. Folklore is also full of portents. As with dreams, much is written to give precise meanings to different occurrences, but often this is not helpful. As with dreams, it is useful sometimes to ask others what such a sign coming at such a time might mean to them, but most likely the individual who notes the sign will already have a pretty good idea of what it means. It is an amazing idea to think that the universe responds in this way, but it really does seem to do so in this synchronistic manner. Once again, respect and attention seem to be determining factors in having seeming randomness replaced by meaningful occurrences. And we have to learn how to "live in the question"—to ask that we be told what we need to know.

David M. Guss also wrote about the widely held belief in the past—and still in many places—that what we think we see of an animal is a disguise that the animal later takes off when "at home." Also, he mentions the understanding that hunters do not outwit and slaughter an animal, but court it. The animal then chooses to give itself up in return for gifts, respect, future power, and an honored death so that in the spirit world it will report favorably on the hunter's generosity. The Ainu of Japan have developed this relationship in their bear cult, where cubs are treated as children until time for their send-off to the next world.

Many hunting societies have shared the code of conduct of respect for what they hunt and consider that the animal is giving the gift of its life rather than having it taken by a hunter's skill or cunning. This view is held by both Native American tribes and Australian Aborigines and was used by Marlo Morgan as part of the message of her novel *Mutant Message Down Under*.

There are many books, including those by Ted Andrews and Jamie Sams, to help with understanding what the presence of certain animals in our lives may mean. Bears are close to us in many ways, yet have skills that we do not have. By hibernating they seem to have a special understanding of the Underworld. They are named among our constellations. The nurturing mother is often symbolized by a bear image. Winnie the Pooh and the teddy bear are beloved childhood companions. Bears are interwoven in our lives, thoughts, and literature. King Arthur's name means "bear." *The Sacred Paw: The Bear in Nature, Myth, and Literature* by Paul Shepard and Barry Sanders is a fine overview of what "bear" means to us and is a model for a rounded way to look at any aspect of nature.

Animals most consider as "pests" can become something quite other. We enjoyed seeing a groundhog and her baby emerge from under a backyard shed in the spring and play on the ramp in the sun. These are gentle creatures and we have seen a groundhog, squirrels, chipmunks, and birds all many times together harmoniously eating sunflower seeds under the bird feeder. We were not so happy to find that a groundhog had a special taste for phlox, which we were hoping to grow in several places. But we tried to communicate and I had the delightful experience of doing this and then seeing a groundhog hold up for my inspection and then eat a sprig of goutweed, which I had suggested since we have an overabundance of it, thanks to a previous owner of this land. We also found that we could enclose prize phlox plants in circles of wire fencing, not enough to really deter a creature, but apparently enough to give a sign of "mouths off," and we were pleased that these signs were honored. We had not seen any groundhogs for a time. Gunshots at dusk one fall some houses away made us wonder if other neighbors had not known how to appreciate these gentle creatures, to everyone's loss. But the next spring a groundhog poked its head out from under the shed and that sighting made us happy.

In *Magical Child Matures* Joseph Chilton Pearce called nature's goal the ability to abstract and create—served by the function of storytelling. Animal-human interactions, he said, dominate folklore and myth. "Animal imagery is the key to this stage of bonding with the earth and to the development of intuition, since our animal brains must be brought into alignment and harmony with our unfolding new, or human, brain."[4] Paul Shepard, in his books *Thinking Animals* and *The Others*, describes how the development of human intelligence, the learning processes of children, our social relationships as adults, and our humanness have depended on our relationship to animals.

So many childhood stories revolve around animals: *The Wind in the Willows, Lassie Come Home, Black Beauty*, and *Charlotte's Web* could start a long list. In *Rascal* Sterling North made a raccoon famous. And at the present time there is an outpouring of writing about personal experiences with other treasured pets and how much their people learned from them.

People sometimes consider themselves to be a glorified part of the animal kingdom, but we are truly dependent on our brothers and sisters whom we may perceive as "other" but who are also part of that kingdom—among all my relations, as some Native Americans say. The moving shamanic paintings of Susan Seddon Boulet, a Brazilian-born artist who lived and worked in California, express our interconnection, with human faces emerging within the bodies of "other" animal beings.

In *Kinship with All Life* J. Allen Boone shared his life-changing experience of getting to know the dog Strongheart as a fellow being, an intelligent and loving expression of the Mind of the Universe. Boone began to realize the great number of good qualities that Strongheart purely expressed and came to feel that all creatures, unless spoiled by humankind, had similar fine qualities and were, unlike many human beings, without deceit and ready for friendship. After Boone came to think of the dog as a fellow being, Strongheart became his teacher and friend and they were able to communicate in silence.

Boone's book strikes a chord of truth with many who have known animals as fellow beings, equal at least to themselves and sometimes superior in noble qualities, and with capabilities that are sometimes beyond their own. In *Pygmalion* the idea is expressed that a lady is "how she is treated," and that thought applies to creatures too. Boone was told to read to Strongheart, to treat him always as an intelligent being, and never to say anything with his mouth that he did not mean in his heart. If you treat an animal with respect and friendship and as a fellow expression of the Creator, your attitude will help to bring forth into your awareness those fine qualities already there in the animal, although formerly perhaps unseen. And you may then be able to help those now seen qualities to blossom.

Boone spoke about the difference in viewing poisonous snakes between the usual White Man and the Native American: the White Man's fear and hate and desire to kill called forth a venomous attack, while the Native American and the snake just noticed each other courteously as each went its own way. Creatures often "are" as they are treated.

11
Air

ALTHOUGH THOSE living in Vermont experience clean air much of the time, most have seen the effects of acid rain and sometimes noticed a very unpleasant air smell from paper mills or industrial sites far away. Toxic residues from jet planes flying overhead fall onto the earth and waterways. When a neighbor uses a toxic spray on lawn or garden, residues may travel with the wind. Seeds from genetically altered plants may blow onto land where they are not wanted. Devastating potato and tomato blight spread quickly with the winds; a recent experience with blight here brought some small understanding of the much greater devastation of a similar potato blight that from 1845 to 1849 in Ireland caused so much starvation and emigration. Everything is connected, and there are consequences to all that everyone does in our earth home.

The work of Al Gore and others after him, including now young Greta Thunberg from Sweden, to make potential effects of global warming known is finally getting some attention, and we are hopeful that there will be real progress in lessening our very large human contributions to disastrous climate change. But there are still a great many people, preoccupied with politics, personal lives, economic issues, and the devastating Covid-19 crisis, who seem oblivious to the serious consequences of complacency and inaction in meeting the climate change danger to the future of our planet home and its inhabitants. We have been part of many Vermont Earth Institute programs, but unfortunately these local

Air

gatherings seem to be "preaching to the converted," for not many beyond our core group have shared in these readings and discussions that have been open to all. There is occasional public lip service to the need to make drastic changes in living practices, but comparatively few people across the country are yet thinking about this in other than a superficial way. And to be fair, even among those aware of the issues, few people know what they can do about any of it except to vote, change their light bulbs, keep their thermostats lower, and drive their cars less often, especially if they have limited funds and are not in positions of political or financial power. We must do what we can, for even small acts do count; but most of all, we need to do everything that we can do to help to change—to enlarge—consciousness.

Weather is a manifestation of air that is part of our daily lives, despite our being cushioned from it by buildings, heating devices, and air conditioners. It is good to become more aware of weather as our wild brethren must, and to learn to take pleasure in its changes of vista and the different feelings of being outside in rain or snow or wind. And, instead of complaining about weather that is inconvenient for our plans, it is good to remember the needs of others. Those with groundwater wells or farms need rain. The Hopis have a prayer for big winter snows so that their summer crops will grow well: in Vermont snow is known as the poor man's fertilizer. Lightning is necessary to revivify the earth, as native peoples are aware.

But weather disasters clearly seem to be proliferating. Worldwide tsunamis, earthquakes, flooding of huge areas, tornadoes, excessive snow and cold, and excessive heat and fires are frequent news these days, with the vast human and creature suffering that follow (although not much is told us in news reports about the suffering of the creatures). It would appear that there are more and more signs of imbalance emerging from the ways in which the earth has been treated and organized by human beings. Many still think in largely mechanistic terms and have the notion that scientific intelligence will solve any problems that human beings create, but some of us think with Nasr that science, accompanied by "the destruction of the sacred and spiritual value of nature," and without integration into "a higher form of knowledge," is often off course and are concerned that only band-aid solutions may be forthcoming because of those limitations. Changes in mainstream consciousness are required—a whole new way of relating to our world and all its inhabitants.

Over time there have been many attempts (such as cloud seeding) to control the weather by technological means. Like many other things that human beings do without really knowing the ramifications of their actions, I feel that this is not the way that we are meant to behave. It may not be that we aren't able to do this in a limited way, but rather that we do not know enough about the possible consequences of our actions: think of the effect of a butterfly's wings on weather across the world as we have become aware of this through chaos theory. Some areas where weather-altering experiments have been carried out have been devastated. The hubris of some human approaches is different from the humility of native rain dances or other shamanic or prayerful means in which the intent is not to force human will on nature but to ask the forces of nature for their help.

On that note, if weather is your friend, it does seem all right, for example, if permission is received, to request that the wind spare a particularly vulnerable tree. I like to include with any such request the qualification, "if it be God's will," as a double-check on my dowsing of permissions, because with even a modest request I cannot know all of the ramifications of what is being asked.

If weather is your friend, you can play with it. I remember a delightful afternoon on a dock on Frenchman's Bay in Maine, watching clouds go overhead and asking if they would like to show us shapes. For about an hour we sat entranced as one figure after another passed by, each more artistically fanciful than the one before.

Windforest by Ellen Fremedon is a reminder that wind is essential to life and that through its movement life and life's by-products are shared. "The microscope," she says, "will show bits of pollen that were originally released to the wind in central Africa, the upper Amazon basin, and southeastern Australia."[1]

Lyall Watson's *Heaven's Breath: A Natural History of the Wind* shows how winds are essential to life, providing circulatory and nervous systems for the planet and bringing life to areas that would otherwise be barren.

> Without wind, most of Earth would be uninhabitable. The tropics would grow so unbearably hot that nothing could live there, and the rest of the planet would freeze. Moisture, if any existed, would be confined to the oceans, and all but the fringe of the great continents along a narrow temperate belt would be desert. There would be no erosion, no soil, and for any community that managed to evolve despite these rigours, no relief from suffocation by their own waste products.[2]

Watson's book includes sections on the physics, the geography, the history, the future, the biology, the sociology, the physiology, the perception, the psychology, and the philosophy of wind, and closes with a dictionary of almost four hundred worldwide names for winds.

Watson reminds us that "Without air, there would be no sound."[3] There are very subtle sounds that the wind makes that only some can hear, and Watson says that the bullroarer, usually a thin board on a cord whirled about the head that makes a sound like the wind, is used by Australian Aborigines (who call it the "master of thunder"), in West Africa, in the Amazon, and by some Native Americans to summon the wind or in rainmaking ceremonies.

Air

Tibetans call their tantric initiations a word meaning wind or breath, referring to the transmission of sacred sounds bearing both knowledge and elemental energies.

Navajo prayers and songs carry the sounds "out of which reality and beauty arise." These are aural patterns expressing "the energy of life and the awareness of mind."[4] The Navajo people understand material reality to have its origin in the partnership of Holy Wind and Universal Mind, together composing the state of being known as Beauty, shown as the summit of the sacred mountain toward which the spiritual hero or heroine travels and from which he or she then returns to the world.

We need air to breathe and are dependent upon it. But there are many subtleties that can be learned about what this means. Many spiritual traditions offer training in breathing practices that are intended to result in changes in consciousness. Also, we can learn to breathe as though we are in a tranquil, beautiful place when we are in a noisy, unpleasant one. Breathing techniques can be helpful in healing and are part of the information in *Meditation as Medicine: Activate the Power of Your Natural Healing Force* by Dharma Singh Khalsa, MD, and Cameron Stauth. And finally, as awareness of our spiritual connection grows, we may come to realize that we are all being breathed.

12

The World of Birds

THE SIGN of a human being really "tuned in" is said to be that he or she is able to understand the language of the birds, also sometimes referred to as the language of the angels. This idea comes through myth, folklore, spiritual accounts, alchemy, and literature. The ability is said to come from God or sometimes through magic, depending on the writer. James Frazer said that this knowledge came from magic rings, magic plants, and from serpents. It was thought that to eat snake or fern seed (sometimes considered to be blood of the sun) would bring about this knowledge. However else it is understood, the language of the birds is a secret language that only some can understand. Solomon was one of those said to know it.

In Kabbalah and alchemy the language of the birds was secret and considered to be the "Green Language." It allowed special information to be communicated only within the inner group.

One of the sets of meanings of ogham alphabets given in *The Book of Ballymote* is bird ogham. Since Robert Graves wrote *The White Goddess*, many think of the Irish ogham alphabet only by its first three tree names, birch-rowan-alder, but ogham has other equivalents as well, including bird ogham with its first three names being pheasant-duck-seagull. A code could be made by knowing all the equivalents, and so people could communicate in a way only understood by those also in the know.

I mentioned before the decoding of Attar's name, suggesting *The Parliament of the Birds* (or *The Conference of the*

Birds), the title of his best-known work. That story is of thousands of birds on a quest to visit the Simurgh, a series of ordeals that leave most of the birds behind and show many of them with all-too-human excuses. In the end thirty arrive at their goal and discover that *si-murgh* means "thirty birds"—themselves.

Birds have symbolized and are often equated with and represent the soul, especially in art. They are sometimes thought of as angels and sometimes considered as psychopomps, communicating with heaven or with the next world. Shamans have a strong affinity with birds and flight and often have worn cloaks of feathers, sometimes were even said to sprout feathers themselves. Suibhne in the *Buile Suibhne* is such a figure. At Lascaux a shaman figure wears what appears to be a bird mask, and a staff is topped by a bird head.

Edward A. Armstrong's *The Folklore of Birds* is a fascinating and well-illustrated study of legends and the magic and religious symbolism of birds throughout the world from ancient times to the present. Among its studies are the history of the eagle and an analysis of the curious (and repellent) hunting of the wren on Saint Stephen's Day (December 26).

Another book offering a great deal of information about everything esoteric you can imagine about birds is *The Secret Language of Birds* by Adele Nozedar. Did you know that on Saint Valentine's Day, if a girl sees a goldfinch, she will marry a wealthy man; if a blue bird, someone poor; a blackbird, a clergyman; a robin, a sailor; a woodpecker, nobody at all? This large, handsome book is a treasury of myths, folklore, and true stories.

The Birds of Heaven is Peter Matthiessen's book on cranes. The red-crowned cranes of Hokkaido have been thought of both as messengers of death and as symbols of eternal life, portrayed by countless artists in a great many media in many lands. Sotatsu's Thousand Crane scroll is echoed in the making of origami cranes, with the thought that if you fold a thousand paper cranes, your heart's desire will be fulfilled. The filmed leaping dance of the red-crowned cranes is a sight never to be forgotten.

A number of books have been written recently about birdsong and how baby birds learn it. In some species it is a learning process; in others, birds seem to hatch already knowing. There is a lot of variety—even dialects—among usual calls, and if attention is paid, sometimes one can get at least an inkling of what is being conveyed. I hope that you will read or study with an animal communicator so that this rich possibility may become open to you. Amelia Kinkade's books are a good place to begin, and I suggest starting with *The Language of Miracles*.

In *The Secret Language of Life* Brian J. Ford reminds us that birds can recognize individuals and outsiders by their songs and their regional accents. Nozedar says that 300 different calls of crows have been noted.

The sense of sight in many birds is extraordinary. Large eagles, for example, see three times as well as we do. Birds see in color, and they can perceive forms of light that we cannot, although nocturnal species see less well than day-flying birds. Many birds are sensitive to the earth's magnetic field. The hoopoe, the messenger who told Solomon about the Queen of Sheba, was thought to be able to forecast the weather by recognizing piezoelectric charges in the atmosphere up to ten hours before the storms or earthquakes that they heralded.

Birds may not hear notes as high as those we can hear, but they can hear notes that are lower. The lower vibrations travel farther. Ford points out that for us to study birdsong we have to plot it on a phonogram or slow it on a tape recorder to understand its complexity, but that birds can notice these distinctions as they listen to one another.

Birds assist farmers by eating many harmful insects. And if their morning songs open the stomata of leaves to receive nutrients, those songs may be very important for plant growth.

Many portents have to do with bird calls and with ornithomancy—divination through the flight of birds and the direction of their flight. Some sign meanings come handed down through folklore: for example, a seagull is sometimes thought to house the soul of a dead mariner.

The strangest bird portent I ever saw was once, when driving toward Burlington near Westfield, Vermont, well away from the sea or indeed any body of water, we saw what appeared to be a pelican. Adele Nozedar suggests that the pelican has been associated with self-sacrifice, unity, and oneness with its flock. Sight of the pelican came after an ice storm had been very damaging to our area, but after which also a strong sense of mutual cooperation and unity had been shown.

Once, a little before a class about Khidr to be held here at our house, we had noticed at the feeder a little redpoll that did not seem well. We were talking about what we should do because we were concerned that it had an illness that had been reported in the news as very contagious to other birds, but we had to stop thinking about this because people were arriving. Then, just before the class started, out of the blue flew down a Cooper's hawk, who pounced on the little bird and killed it in a single blow, then strutted about a bit so that we could see it clearly before it seized the dead bird and flew off with it. When you read more about Khidr in the chapter on the Green Man you will understand what this meant to us.

A sign to me to pay attention has been the call of a loon, in past years heard occasionally coming from our wooded back yard. We are quite far from any body of water, and it seems remote that a loon would be flying from pond to pond, here quite a distance apart. When I have heard the loon it has been a single call from the wooded hill behind our house and usually it has meant to me a "heads up" for something that I was meant to notice and then did, because of the call. Once, however, I felt it was simply a message of encouragement, and when I researched the shamanic understanding of the loon, that kind of support message was confirmed. Now is this loon a supernatural bird? I think not. But does its natural call sometimes also have a special meaning—and perhaps not only for me? I think yes to both.

A public television offering, *A Murder of Crows*, was about studies that show crows as tool users, joining chimpanzees and elephants as well as human beings with that distinction. This film expressed a new awareness of crow intelligence and showed crows apparently thinking out solutions to problems and adapting what was available as tools to do what was needed.

Doctor Louis Lefebvre at McGill University has compiled an avian IQ index. Corvids top the list, followed by hawks and falcons, herons and woodpeckers. At least one researcher has said that average bird IQ is 135, while the average human intelligence is 100. The "bird brain" slur needs to be rethought.

In *Dawn Light* Diane Ackerman wrote about her friend Kyllikki's starling named Sprinkle. Starlings are among the birds that can mimic language, but it appears that what happened with Sprinkle—and with other birds we've read about—is more than that. A friend who knows Kyllikki told us that Sprinkle had watched her owner looking into the mirror and had said regretfully, "Too bad you don't have a beak." At another time when someone complained of a headache, Sprinkle advised, "Take an aspirin."

Homing pigeons were a great help to the Allies during World War II. As the Pigeon Post, they carried messages back and forth between Europe and Buckingham Palace. Two hundred thousand pigeons were involved in the Allies' cause. One pigeon named Snow White flew through Berlin during bombardments and was awarded the Military Cross. About thirty birds received the Dicken Medal for bravery.

In contrast to this we remember in this country the mindless slaughter for "sport" of the passenger pigeons, once a huge number, now extinct.

I hope you know Paul Gallico's beautiful story *The Snow Goose*. The hero of the story is a humpbacked and crippled painter who lives in isolation and cares for wounded migrating birds. The wounded snow goose is brought to him by a young girl, and over the years the three form an unspoken bond. When the painter learns of the impending tragedy at Dunkirk, he sets sail in his little boat to ferry soldiers from the beaches to the large transport ships. The snow goose, flying above him, becomes a symbol of love and hope to all the men who see her.

Although we have all heard of the wonders of bird migration, nothing could bring the power of that home more clearly than the magnificent film (and DVD) *Winged Migration*. It would be impossible to see that without amazement at the kingdom of the birds and what they are able to accomplish—and do—year in and year out. I can't imagine anyone seeing that film and not recognizing that there is meaning and purpose in all of creation.

In an animal communication session I questioned the hummingbird oversoul, a kind of group soul for the species. I asked how hummingbirds knew when to fly south; the answer received was that the taste of the nectar changes. I asked, weren't their long journeys very exhausting; the answer, not exhausting like they could be—because the air beings sometimes carried them when they needed help.

13

THE WORLD OF INSECTS

IN *THE Voice of the Infinite in the Small,* Joanne Elizabeth Lauck shows that, although our belief that many insects are adversaries to be eradicated is deep-seated, this is an unquestioned assumption that does not stand up to the facts. Saint Colman in *Beasts and Saints* had a fly that sat on his holy books to keep his place on the line when he was called away. And although it surprised people that in *Kinship with All Life* J. Allen Boone wrote of befriending a fly, Lauck shows time and again that the insect world responds to consciousness and good intent.

Lauck tells of the Perelandra garden and how Machaelle Small Wright made a pact with the insect world, leaving a few plants at the ends of rows for them while asking that the rest of the plants be left alone, which the insects did. Realizing the pain of the Japanese beetles for being so hated, she decided not even to make any requests of them, but found that they responded to her beneficent intent anyway so that a balance was attained.

When we find individual insects and spiders in the house we try to scoop them up, using a plastic cup and a file card, and take them outside.

With quantities of insects a different method is needed. Our friend Lydia Jastram spoke to the group soul of the earwigs and requested that an infestation of earwigs leave her house, and this she said they did. Terry Ross requested that no spruce budworms come onto his land and they didn't, although they were widespread in the area where he lived. In making requests that they move, if possible suggest a place to which the insects are welcome to go.

In *Mutant Message Down Under* Marlo Morgan wrote of the bushflies that her major character thought were a terrible pest, climbing over her body and into her nose and ears, but she was taught by one of her Aboriginal companions that they were performing a great service in cleaning her and should be appreciated. A change in perspective made all the difference in how they were viewed.

Boll weevils in an area in Alabama were later honored by the community with a monument after a severe infestation in cotton fields caused some farmers to diversify their crops and so return to prosperity, as other nearby farmers unfortunately did not.

Although there are many less harmful ways than pesticides to control insect populations, the thought behind Lauck's book is that if the human being stays out of the equation, natural checks and balances will prevail, but that where we disrupt the food chain there will be trouble that will only increase. Even for diseases like malaria, Lauck says that our mosquito eradication attempts have had a long-range effect opposite to that desired.

Lauck's book is very interesting reading in support of the understanding that all the kingdoms have intelligence and an essential role to play and that we discount to our peril the importance of even the smallest creature as part of a healthy ecosystem.

When we have talked about the Lauck book in a group I have also brought in a copy of *The Art of Annemieke Mein*. She is a wildlife textile artist, born in Holland but now an Australian citizen, who has paid real attention to the insect world, as reflected in her intricate and beautiful embroideries.

Choices for Sustainable Living mentions that a recent survey by the World Wildlife Fund noted that the bees that pollinate a Costa Rican farmer's crop and the nearby forest are "worth" as much as sixty thousand dollars annually to the farmer. Also it is estimated that a sixty-billion-a-year chunk of the U.S. economy is supported by wild bugs. It is time that creatures viewed so often as pests are instead understood to be important, not only in their own right, but to us as well. If we did not have their help in pollination, can you imagine what that would mean to the world?

A strong memory of my childhood was watching fireflies in huge numbers. Where we now live a neighbor on the hillside above us for many years had a bug zapper and we would hear the ugly sound it made as it exterminated everything that it attracted. Now we see only an occasional firefly.

A PBS film on monarch butterflies revealed current understanding of one of the mysteries of insect life. These frail and handsome butterflies fly sometimes thousands of miles from eastern parts of Canada and the United States to a small area in Mexico where they overwinter. This small area is being impacted by logging by people who feel that they must log in order to live, so that naturalists are very concerned about the future fate of these butterflies. The monarchs who fly to this winter spot are not the ones who will make the trip again; those are monarchs four generations later. How they do this is unknown, but on the crowded "butterfly trees" millions of monarchs congregate.

Brian Ford in *The Secret Language of Life* points out that many insects form complex social communities, some like a single organism with individuals contributing to the good of the whole. Ants and bees come immediately to mind as creatures who act together as units.

An Austrian scientist, Karl von Frisch, revealed the astonishing waggling dance of the honeybees that communicates the direction and source of food. Although the waggle dance is universal among honeybees, different strains of bees exhibit slight differences, just as bird calls vary slightly from place to place. It seems that it is variations in air pressure created by the dance of the bees that reveal the messages even in the dark.

14

WATER

*We can't help being thirsty,
moving toward the voice of water.*

—Rumi, version by Coleman Barks[1]

TWO THIRDS of the surface of the earth is covered by water, and water makes up a very large percentage of the human body. Water is absolutely essential to life as we know it: human beings must have water to drink, for cooking and bathing, to germinate seeds, and to keep alive plants and animals for their own sake as well as because some of them are human food. And yet, although we are so dependent on water and treat it so casually, water is more mysterious than most people know.

In our society, instead of treating water as an important and sacred substance, we waste it and pollute it with sewage and chemical run-off. We think of what water does and can do for us, but seldom do we consider water's own nature and purpose. We may be annoyed and fearful when we don't have it as in times of drought, but few of us are daily grateful for its blessing.

A way to begin to become more aware of the nature of water is to read about the work of Viktor Schauberger, an Austrian forester who, living for many years in close proximity to water, began to learn its secrets. He found that on clear cold nights, at four degrees Celsius, water has its greatest carrying capacity, so that logs then could most easily be floated downstream. To straighten their banks harms watercourses;

for water's health water needs to meander. And vegetation should not be cut from the banks, for shade on the water is also necessary for water's health. Healthy water is living water, but water can die. Metal pipes harm water, Schauberger thought, so that water needs to be transported in stone or wood, with a vein that turns the water inside the pipe to create vortex movement. By Schauberger's criteria most of the water consumed today lacks the life force with which he was concerned. Olof Alexandersson and Callum Coats have written about his work, and there are also excellent books by Alick Bartholomew: *Hidden Nature: The Startling Insights of Viktor Schauberger* and *The Spiritual Life of Water*.

Others have worked to find ways to return the life force to water, some basing their research on Hunza water coming from a remote valley surrounded by the highest Himalayan peaks. Tompkins and Bird tell in *Secrets of the Soil* how in the 1920s a Romanian, Henry Coanda, discovered that a liquid flowing over a surface tends to cling as though it is alive. Using the Huyck Research Lab in Connecticut, Coanda studied Hunza water in its crystalline form as snowflakes. Using a fluid amplifier he invented that could make snow from water, he found that in the center of each flake is a circulatory system of tiny tubes in which still unfrozen water circulates like sap in plants. The snowflakes die when all the water has become congealed. It seemed that the longer lasting snowflakes made of Hunza water correlated with the Hunza people's longer life span. Later Coanda turned over his research to Patrick Flanagan.

According to Flanagan, water constitutes 90 percent of the human brain, and water, the universal solvent, is capable in time of dissolving even gold. Water grows lighter as it freezes, has surface tension so that it sticks to itself, and forms a spherical shape with the least amount of surface for its volume, so requiring the least amount of energy to maintain itself. Yet its potential strength is great. Were all the extraneous gases to be removed from an inch-thick column of water, Flanagan says, that column would become harder than steel. We remember from the *Tao Te Ching*, "Under heaven nothing is more soft and yielding than water. Yet for attacking the solid and strong nothing is better."

Coanda told Flanagan that "We are what we drink," and Flanagan and his wife Gael continued to work toward duplicating Hunza colloidal water. Hunza glaciers yield pure water, but the pressure from millions of tons of ice grinds the minerals in its path. Then vortices in the torrents put charges on the nonsoluble minerals to make them colloidal.

In *Elixir of the Ageless* the Flanagans say that when we are born we are about 97 percent water, about 70 percent at adulthood. "As we age, our bodies harden as we lose the ability to store water. Aging is a slow process of dehydration."[2] In *Your Body's Many Cries for Water* F. Batmanghelidj, MD, says that the primary cause of Alzheimer's disease is dehydration of the body, and giving the body sufficient water, he finds, allows many diseases to disappear.

In *Water: The Element of Life* Theodor and Wolfram Schwenk published photos of drop pictures that show differences in water quality. In *The Divining Heart* we recalled that in his earlier book, *Sensitive Chaos*, "Theodor Schwenk describes how the plant world plays its role in the circulation of water; on a summer's day, he says, 3,500 gallons are 'drawn through an acre of woodland into the atmosphere. . . . Together earth, plant world and atmosphere form a single great organism, in which water streams like living blood.' Animals and people have this same kind of system within themselves 'in a small space, where it moves in just such rhythms and according to just such laws as the water outside in nature.' Schwenk also points out that water, with no 'inherent form of its own,' is yet the 'matrix of all metamorphoses of form.'

(A matrix is that within which and from which something takes form.)"³

Jennifer Greene at her laboratory in Blue Hill, Maine, has worked with the drop picture method developed by Theodore Schwenk. Water, a droplet at a time, is dripped mechanically and recorded in high-speed photographs. This method shows the interrelationship of components that make up water quality and whether technically clean water still lacks important characteristics, and it can identify contaminated water needing testing for specific pollutants. Drop pictures of excellent quality water show upon impact patterns resembling flower petals or leaves.

Rhythmic treatment of water toward its rehabilitation has been one of Greene's studies, using flowforms designed by John Wilkes of England. These forms are designed to give water back its natural forms—to set up rhythms and vortices in the water as it flows through them and to fold air into the water to aerate it. Flowforms are being used now in many countries, not only as decorative waterways but to change the flat taste of desalinized sea water to that of a mountain stream and to deodorize sewage lagoons. Water quality has been shown to be improved by this rhythmic treatment.

John Todd and his wife Nancy Jack Todd were instrumental in founding the New Alchemy Institute on Cape Cod and later Ocean Arks International, and the Todds and their colleagues have designed miniature water ecosystems, including food producing systems, and have developed new approaches to processing sewage and industrial waste using microorganisms, algae, fish, and other living creatures, replicating and accelerating the natural purification processes of streams, ponds, and marshes. Nature's way has been the teacher.

It is not yet well known that water is affected by consciousness, by thought. In June 1988 *Nature* published the finding of four scientists—from France, Canada, Israel, and Italy, and including Professor Jacques Benveniste—that implied that antibodies in the immune system can function even when the solution they are in is so diluted that no antibody molecules are left: as though the solution were able to remember the antibody molecules that had been there. There was no known basis for such a physical action, and the study was of course of great interest in terms of suggesting how homeopathy may work.

In homeopathy a small amount of a substance is diluted and shaken, acquiring greater potency the more times this is done, so that there is less and less of the original matter in the mixture. Homeopathy works on the principle of "like cures like," and it seems that a very dilute substance of a material that could have caused the patient's symptoms, prepared in this way, can act as a catalyst to the body to repair itself. We also suggest that morphic resonance of thought-forms built up through particular usages over time may help to account for the results obtained.

Massimo Citro's *The Basic Code of the Universe: The Science of the Invisible in Physics, Medicine, and Spirituality* gives several theories explaining homeopathy and says that "water is able to receive, retain, and return information because it fluctuates between coherent and noncoherent states" and that "water carrying the appropriate information can act on the body's fluids in order to help return them to a coherent state. This might be a homeopathic remedy or any other 'informed' water."[4] This book also describes a new method of Transfer Pharmacological Frequency (TFF) where the information of a medicine is transferred into water for later administration to an organism.

As a dowser, I am familiar with the affinity of thought and water. It has been known for many years that, once a dowser has reached a certain level of experience and consciousness, after a request that is thought alone, a water vein may be shown to have moved. Water appears to be able to be detoxified through thought too. And as dowsers we have long speculated that healing through prayer (thought) may be brought about through the medium of water within the body.

Thus it was not a new idea that Masaru Emoto's photographs of ice crystals show beautiful crystals when water had been exposed to beautiful thoughts and misshapen crystals when it had been exposed to ugly thoughts. And his photographs, as did the drop pictures previously mentioned, show pure water with lovely crystals and polluted water with distorted crystals. Emoto's work, although sometimes criticized for lacking in scientific rigor, has become a popular way for people to see for themselves the effects of both positive and negative thoughts, and as such it is welcome. But dowsers have long known that a thought is a thing, or as Larry Dossey, MD, has put it: "mind and body are intrinsically united, and consciousness is the fulcrum of health."[5]

Citro comments that "conviction starts transformation at a cellular level. . . . Or you can inform water, modifying its structure, so that it carries the message."[6] He feels that ritual is necessary to carry conviction and because a doctor must give something. Conviction, accompanied by imagination and visualization, can transform matter. Since our bodies contain such a high percentage of water, the water in the cellular makeup of the body can be imprinted by the mind with positive thoughts toward wellness. "The key is to believe intensely and absolutely. This allows the conviction to start and to become a force that does not recede, not even in light of evidence to the contrary. 'If you believe and do not doubt,' says Jesus. The Indian teacher Paramahamsa Yogananda wrote, 'The world is only an objectified dream, and anything your powerful mind believes intensely occurs instantly.'"[7]

A thought is a thing, and the thoughts of patient and medical personnel and family and friends all have an effect and are crucial. All our thoughts go out from us and affect the world, so it is important that they not be worries and fears or in any way negative, but instead be positive thoughts and blessings. Many also believe that the thoughts we send out return to affect us.

As well as noting the benefits of positive thoughts on water, we need to remember that negative thoughts also can have an effect—and that water's memory means that sometimes harm may be held in that memory.

Dowsers have discovered that some water veins under buildings may cause discomfort and harm to some individuals living over them. My personal understanding of this is that sometimes water picks up harmful thoughts or emanations and holds and concentrates them. Sometimes this seems to be when nearby chi lines have become blocked and have thus become harmful. (For more about dowsing and harmful effects of some water veins, please read *The Divining Heart*.) Water veins causing problems may be moved or detoxified in a variety of ways, but both of these results may be brought about through a request that is both thought and prayer.

Awareness of water veins and other earth energies is valuable for architects and builders to acquire because of course it is better to build in harmony with the land rather than to have to repair damage that has been done through lack of this knowledge.

15

The World of Fish and Other Water Creatures

I THINK FIRST of the Irish salmon of wisdom, Fintan, fed on the magic hazelnuts that fell into the water where the salmon lived. When this fish was caught and was being cooked, Finn touched it, put his burned finger into his mouth, and thereby attained wisdom. A cooked fish coming back to life and swimming away at the meeting of the two seas is a motif in a story of Khidr about whom you will read more in the chapter on the Green Man; the two seas represent this world and the world beyond.

Brian J. Ford in *The Secret Language of Life* says that most fish migrate, many navigating by odors and tastes in the water. Many sea fish return to fresh water to lay their eggs; the eel reverses this pattern. Fish can see, smell, and "talk," and can move together in finely tuned choreographies, as do flocks of birds. They also have organs that detect changes in water pressure that tell them about movements of predators or prey and can sense electrical signals from the muscular activities of other water creatures. They can use intelligence to escape predators. Rises in temperature or pollution cause fish to change their navigational patterns. But they are also explorers, which is how salmon and trout return to rivers that have recovered from being ecologically inhospitable. As pets, fish can recognize people and know usual meal times.

In folklore many tales revolve around fish or other denizens of the deep. Reports of dolphin rescues of human beings are found worldwide, and efforts to communicate with dolphins, beginning with John Lilly's accounts, are well known.

Like whales, dolphins have very high intelligence, probably more than our own, and it seems that they have healing skills as well. In *The Secret Life of the Universe*, Amy Corzine tells of the dolphin Fungi living in Dingle Bay off the coast of Ireland, where the sick go to swim with Fungi. The dolphin's sophisticated sonar system can apparently "see" within the body; people have reported feeling scanned. Some scientists, Corzine says, suggest that the dolphin heals human cells with sonar, changing cellular metabolism. She also reports a belief that human brainwaves are altered from beta to theta, improving the immune system and synchronizing the two halves of the brain. Children with developmental disabilities have shown remarkable improvements in learning and cognitive abilities after dolphin therapy. She also says "Dolphin sonar is four times stronger than the ultrasound therapeutically used in hospitals to destroy cataracts, kidney stones and gallstones, and is similar to the drumming, chanting, and music used by ancient cultures to promote good health. Such sounds influence heart rate, breathing, muscle contractions, memory and immune function."[1]

It is lovely to read of this kind of dolphin-human interaction and of the times that dolphins have saved swimmers who might otherwise have drowned. But it is not lovely to think of dolphins being trained for war use or of the many that are caught and killed in commercial fishing nets or trapped in the great masses of plastic trash that, thanks to human beings, the oceans now contain. And there is a very terrible history of human slaughter of enormous numbers of whales.

Jim Nollman has communicated through music with whales and found that they would sing with him. In *The Charged Border: Where Whales and Humans Meet* he describes adventures in four oceans with dolphins and whales. He also refers to severely depressed patients who were bundled into dry suits and dropped into the Irish Sea to swim with dolphins, an act that had immediate effect on their will to live. In the Arctic Nollman's playing of music lured to safety gray whales that had been trapped under the ice.

Many TV cooking shows now feature calamari, but as with the use for food of all creatures and plants, usually nothing is said in thanks to the beings whose lives have been given or taken to continue our own. With increasing book and media attention to the octopus, more people may learn about this spirited and intelligent mollusk. *The Soul of an Octopus: A Surprising Exploration into the Wonder of Consciousness* by Sy Montgomery is a good place to start reading.

The great bounty of the fish world as food for human beings has been spoiled by greed. Many of the past great fishery areas have been depleted, which, in addition to being a terrible way to treat fellow creatures, is like destroying the principal from which interest could come. This has been done by industrialized fishing, scooping up everything, leaving nothing, in much the same way that mindless slaughter of buffalo herds and bird flocks led to extinction or near extinction in the early days of this country. Mark Kurlansky's book *Cod* is an elegant elegy for that "fish that changed the world."

This kind of madness is what Paul Shepard addressed in his book *Nature and Madness* as the situation in society to which failure of what nature intended to be our natural development has led. The Atlantic fisheries have been affected for some time, but now we are learning also of the great lessening of the Pacific salmon. We still have not learned the lesson although it has been repeated many times, which brings to mind the story that to encourage attention one first is given a tap on the shoulder, then a push, and finally a hit with a big stick. We seem to be moving fast toward requiring the big stick.

One of our spring pleasures has been the raucous nightly calling of spring peepers in our little pond. My husband sometimes played his double native flute with these tiny frogs, and it was a delight to have them listen to his contribution and then respond, playing back and forth as true musicians improvising together will do.

Brian Ford mentions that frogs have dialects and that their ears are attuned to the different frequencies, allowing them to home in on the calls of prospective mates. Amphibians seem able to orient themselves toward home by the position of the sun, and some by that of stars and the moon. Frogs seem able to smell their home ponds.

A lovely story is told in *My Grandfather's Blessings* by Rachel Naomi Remen, MD. An old man is walking along a beach, gently throwing back into the water starfish stranded on the sand by the ebbing tide. A passing jogger laughs at him for thinking he is making a difference; the jogger reminds him of the enormous number of starfish on the sand, not only there but on many other beaches of the world, and that there will be other ebb tides. The jogger runs on. The old man continues with what he was doing. As he gently throws another starfish back into the ocean, he says to himself, "Made a difference to that one."

16

ART

TO CONSIDER art in its relationship to spirituality and to nature, it seems appropriate to begin with some traditional views.

In *Sacred Art in East and West* Titus Burckhardt says that "spirituality in itself is independent of forms." He goes on, however, to say that "Through its qualitative essence form has a place in the sensible order analogous to that of truth in the intellectual order.... Every sacred art is therefore founded on a science of forms, or in other words, on the symbolism inherent in forms."[1]

Ananda Coomeraswamy says in *Christian and Oriental Philosophy of Art* that, with the exception of the monk, people are idlers who are not artists in some field. The kind of artist to become is up to the individual, and we are reminded that primitive man did not distinguish between sacred and secular: everything should be done in the same spirit, and all possessions must be both beautiful and useful. Since all things are related to metaphysical concepts, superficial resemblances of art to nature are not what is to be sought. Instead of copying a fern frond, one must look for what forms the fern frond.

Burckhardt says that in the Christian view the divine image is the human form of the Christ, with Christian art having as its purpose the transfiguration of man and of the world, while the Islamic view is universal and impersonal, with divine art manifesting the unity and regularity of the cosmos. In the Taoist view, nature is ceaselessly being transformed;

Art

one who understands the circular movement recognizes the center that is its essence. The Buddha's beauty expresses a state beyond thought, reflected in the lotus and perpetuated in images of the Buddha.

In *Islamic Art and Spirituality* Seyyed Hossein Nasr wrote:

> Islamic art is the result of the manifestation of Unity upon the plane of multiplicity.... This art makes manifest, in the physical order directly perceivable by the senses, the archetypal realities and acts, therefore, as a ladder for the journey of the soul from the visible and the audible to the Invisible which is also Silence transcending all sound.... Islamic art does not imitate the outward forms of nature but reflects their principles.[2]

In the Islamic tradition the pen is used to signify divine creation and so calligraphy is an important art form. It is said that as Christ is to Christianity, the Qur'an is to Islam. The Qur'an stands for the book of nature, and the mosque is meant to represent the forest and virgin nature and also hint at the gates of paradise. The mihrab, the prayer niche in the mosque dedicated to Mary, represents the gates of paradise, and this is also a motif repeated on many prayer carpets, along with the flowers of paradise.

Nasr comments that the universe can also be symbolized by a tree and so calligraphic words are combined with plant forms known as arabesques. The geometric forms in Islamic art represent immutable patterns, while the arabesques are related to life and growth. As suggested before, the books of Keith Critchlow are helpful guides to understanding this art form.

In *The Mysteries of Chartres Cathedral* Louis Charpentier refers to the star maps traced on the ground through the placement of Christian cathedrals and abbeys, as is also seen in the mapping of earlier stone sites in England. The geometry of Chartres and its relationship to alchemy and the grail are detailed in this book. The colors of the stained glass, which it is not known now how to duplicate, are those seen in the development of the alchemical Great Work. As in Islamic architecture, there are many messages in the building that may be decoded by those who know.

The Navajo conception of Beauty was mentioned as the summit of the spiritual mountain of ascent. Irish Catholic John O'Donohue in *Beauty: The Invisible Embrace* wrote of "the eternal beauty which presides over all the journeys between awakening and surrender, the visible and the invisible, the light and the darkness." He says that "In a sense, all the contemporary crises can be reduced to a crisis about the nature of beauty." He continues,

> Perhaps, for the first time, we gain a clear view of how much ugliness we endure and allow. The media generate relentless images of mediocrity and ugliness in talk-shows, tapestries of smothered language and frenetic gratification. The media are becoming the global mirror and these shows tend to enshrine the ugly as the normal standard. Beauty is mostly forgotten and made to seem naïve and romantic. The blindness of property development creates rooms, buildings and suburbs which lack grace and mystery. Socially, this influences the atmosphere in the workplace, the schoolroom, the boardroom and the community. It also results in such degradation of the environment that we are turning more and more of our beautiful earth into a wasteland. Much of the stress and emptiness that haunts us can be traced back to our lack of attention to beauty. Internally, the mind becomes coarse and dull if it remains unvisited by images and thoughts which hold the radiance of beauty.[3]

O'Donohue says that "We were created to be creators. At its deepest heart, creativity is meant to serve and evoke beauty,"[4] akin to Rumi's thought in the Coleman Barks version:

> Let the beauty we love be what we do.
> There are hundreds of ways to kneel and kiss the ground.[5]

Art

Human beings are not the only beings with a need for creativity and beauty. Books show art created by animals, such as paintings by elephants and chimpanzees and cats. Structures built by dogs are pictured in *Dog Works: The Meaning and Magic of Canine Constructions*. The amazing complexities of many bird nests are beyond human ability to recreate, although some basket weavers try to emulate their techniques. Bowerbirds of Australia build elaborate constructions to attract mates, decorating them with flowers and shells and even "painting" them with fruits and charcoal. Spider webs, considered by some native peoples as the inspiration for and origin of weaving, are often elegant, especially when seen spangled with morning dew.

Photography has helped to make us more aware of the beauties of nature—not only in landscape but in the great variety in coloration of bird plumage and animal coats, the markings on amphibians and fish, the brilliance and design of leaves, flowers, and fungi. A favorite book of mine, *Hidden Art in Nature* by Oscar Forel, shows just the bark of trees in page after page of subtle colors and textures, like the highest form of beauty in Japanese art called "shibui."

Bluejays and cardinals in the snow; the subtleties of reds and golds amid green maple leaves in the fall; rosy bee balm with a hummingbird poised over it; the autumn pink of hills in Vermont beyond a blue lake; the ever-changing cloudscape; formations of Canada geese returning north—such sights remind us that Nature is always the supreme artist.

The courtship rituals of many creatures have now been filmed, none more elegant than the dance of the red-crowned cranes of the Hokkaido region of Japan. The choreography is breathtaking, with the cranes taking great leaps into the air and moving together in what appears as a well-rehearsed ballet.

Andy Goldsworthy is probably the best known of ephemeral artists using stones and other natural materials like leaves and sticks. He is from Great Britain, but his works are scattered around the world, where they are left in nature as constructed so that they eventually weather or erode away. Goldsworthy's work has a more permanent form in photographs and books and in a lovely DVD called *Of Rivers and Tides*.

Sometimes, as I described with the clouds in Maine, nature will play art with you. A way to see this is in setting up seaweed or shells along a tide line. Marty Cain, an environmental artist, has shown time-sequenced slides showing changes that playful tides have made to her shore constructions.

Beautiful buildings made with natural materials include primitive shelters, artists' homes, and sophisticated works such as Frank Lloyd Wright's famous Bear Run house, built over a Pennsylvania waterfall. *The Natural Home* and *Handmade Houses* showcase some other examples of beautiful homes. More and more attention is now being paid in home building and renovation to working with natural materials that do not pose hazards to the occupants or to the environment and that are beautiful in themselves.

New energy technologies are being developed to provide heat and electricity as well as to power vehicles, and we hope that these efforts will progress speedily to reduce greenhouse gases and to help to bring economic stability to the world. Although we all are unlikely to be able to purchase the best possibilities in the new housing and energy fields, we can be cognizant of what we can afford and try to make as conscious decisions as we are able for what we do build or buy. This means reading about architecture and energy to try to stay aware of what the emerging possibilities are.

I strongly concur with O'Donohue and Rumi about the centrality of beauty and feel very sad that our society as a whole often does not seem to recognize beauty or to understand its relationship to truth. I am very grateful to have grown up in an ambience in which truth, beauty, and excellence were linked and central. The quandary is how to teach that centrality to people who have not had similar good fortune and who sometimes sadly do not even seem to recognize beauty when it is before them. So many commercial offerings in our time are ugly that that is what many people are used to seeing, and so that ugliness becomes, by unquestioned assumption, the norm.

An answer to that quandary—as to so many puzzles—is to be found in nature. A start is to go into a wild place (or as wild a one as you can easily find), into woods or fields, by the sea or a lake or stream, probably alone unless with very compatible companions, to spend some time just quietly there, observing, letting the peace of the place seep into you. Do this as often as you can. Let thoughts go; if thoughts persist in arising, don't be upset—just let them drift away like leaves moving by on a stream or clouds going by. Just be there in nature, a conscious presence, observing. This is a form of meditation.

At times you can try to get into the consciousness of a tree or a stone or the water or a creature you may see. For example, sit leaning against a tree and feel that you are merging with it; feel your roots going deep into the earth, your crown high into the sky. Relate to the creatures and birds around you, to the sun, or to the moon and stars, to the wind or rain or snow. Feel how it would be to be rooted in one place for many years, a participant, providing shade and shelter, but also an observer. Gradually you may be able to experience something of what it means to be a tree and may even sense the tree experiencing you. Hugging trees has often been reported to elicit feelings of being loved by the trees, potentially a metanoia, an epiphany, a life-changing moment.

A similar kind of identification can be forged with any creature or natural object or element. And as you spend more time immersed in nature, you will begin more and more to notice beautiful things. Nature is God's handiwork that you are seeing—the best that there is.

Fortunately there are also books and museums and occasionally magazines to help to educate us in recognizing beauty. Locate and immerse yourself in the best, which likely will not be the newest fad.

In the early 1960s *House Beautiful* magazine had wonderful issues I still cherish that were devoted to Scandinavian and Japanese design. The Scandinavian issues showed the wooden furniture of Hans Wegner, gorgeous stoneware and glass like that which could be seen then at Georg Jensen and Bonniers in New York, stone boxes with lichen lids, and beautifully embroidered pillow covers. Awareness of such beauty prompted me, after my regular workweek, to clerk on Saturdays for a modern design shop where in any spare moments I pored over catalogs from Denmark, Sweden, and Norway. Also the Japanese-themed issues of *House Beautiful* were really a course in understanding Japanese stages of beauty, culminating in *shibui*—the most subtle use of color and texture. I learned about *shibori*, a fine and complicated form of tie-dye. Interest in small netsuke and inro carvings began then, and I have been able to pursue those interests through books and museums. A wise person once told me that if you have once really seen something, you own it always: you do not have to possess it other than in your memory.

Other *House Beautiful* issues near that time showed houses of Frank Lloyd Wright and airy weavings of Lenore Tawney. Years later the early issues of Threads were inspirational too, for then they were featuring a wide variety of textile craftspeople. And in a more recent *Ornament* magazine an article led me to the handsome book *Kimono as Art: The Landscapes of Itchiku Kuboto*, showing his intricate and subtle shibori textile work in kimono form. Another contemporary artist using shibori in a very different way is Carter Smith, whose work has often been shown in *Ornament*.

But it is rare anymore to see what I consider to be beautiful either in magazines or in the commercial offerings of shops.

The best chance to find beauty now is in the work of individual craftspeople. In his turned wood bowls and vases Mel Lindquist pioneered the use of spalted wood that was starting to decay and had been marked by water in strange and beautiful ways. Mel and his son Mark Lindquist continued their sculptural work, also using burls, and now many other craftspeople use those beautiful but often-before discarded materials.

Woodcarvers use both milled woods and raw found pieces for intricately carved and painted work and, more simply, for letting what is in the wood come forth with just a few chisel strokes. Fine wood carvings of birds like those by northern Vermont artist Jim Maas, more primitive sculptural work like the Saint Francises of Ben Ortega or that shown in *American Vernacular*, and the variety of techniques illustrated in books on bird and fish decoys show a range of possibilities. In Pennsylvania, George Nakashima let the wood speak through his furniture, often using beautifully grained slabs of wood with bark edges showing. Daniel Mack has taught many people how to make rustic furniture using natural materials. Artists Mary Azarian and Sabra Field have produced handsome woodblock prints of Vermont scenes.

Basketry is a tradition with many subtleties and beautiful examples, especially among baskets from the Far East and from native peoples worldwide. Birchbark baskets by Suzanne Nash are among my treasures. Basketry has always made use of reeds, grasses, and barks, and recently there has been a proliferation of intricate work using unusual natural materials in unconventional ways that allow their beauty to be recognized. Sometimes these natural basket materials are used in doll making, as in the work of Akira Blount.

Much beauty comes from clay. I first saw the work of Karen Karnes long ago at America House in New York, and as she became a friend here we were privileged to see the evolution of the craft of this master potter. There is now a beautiful book, *A Chosen Path: The Ceramic Art of Karen Karnes*, showing the history of her work. Malcolm Wright makes beautiful clay pieces in shibui coloring, fired in his Japanese-inspired wood kiln in southern Vermont.

Weaving, felting, rug hooking, appliqué, embroidery, and knitting make use of wool, cotton, and linen—and now many new threads that are made from bamboo, soy, milk, bananas, shells, and even algae. Dyes and pigments come in large part from natural sources, and inspiration for the textile arts often comes from nature. Czechoslovakian fiber artist Luba Krejci made intricate pictures from knotted threads, exhibited long ago in New York, never to be forgotten. Danish artist Birgitte Krag Hansen has created amazing sculptural felted pieces including animals and trees. Japanese artist Ayako Miyawaki's appliqués of the vegetables and fish of her everyday world are a delight. The Fiberarts Design series of books document many contemporary pieces, and there are many inspirational textile design books based on nature, including Constance Howard's *Inspiration for Embroidery* and Verina Warren's *Landscape in Embroidery*.

Flowers, branches, twigs, seed pods, bark, stones, shells, found feathers, and moss all find places in our home. But it seems appropriate to dowse or intuit whether, for example, a stone wishes to remain where it is or whether it would like to come home with you before removing it from where you have found it. Many objects want to stay where they are. I now usually do not cut flowers, but like watching their longer life where they are growing, and for indoor flowers enjoy potted plants.

I cannot imagine life without the pleasure of doing creative work. And both looking at art and creating art are increasingly recognized as healing. What kind of creative work you choose is up to you. You may choose to write. In journal keeping, attention to nature's epiphanies always will provide subject matter. Music offers many possibilities and even new ways to think about music. As mentioned before, a friend learning to play a wooden flute was instructed by her Native American teacher not to play tunes the way she had always done with her silver flute, but instead to play the landscape she was seeing, a very different kind of music.

There are many handcrafts that people can enjoy. Recently I was part of a group of mostly retired men, but a few women too, learning to better wood carve; we all enjoyed the camaraderie of the group and the inspiration we gave each other to do our best—not a contest among us, but each to do an own personal best. More experienced carvers were very gracious with their suggestions and help to the novices, which is true of the way most experienced craftspeople treat beginners.

I have taught beginning textile techniques in schools and community college, and it was always a great pleasure to me to have people, who at the beginning would say that they had no talent or creativity and would have to follow someone else's kit or design, then discover that they could design and do their own work. The joy that accomplishment and realization gave them was real, and I hope heralded continuing pleasure for them. I know that making things always has been a great source of pleasure for me. I still have a favorite childhood book called *The Critter Book* by Ellen Simon that encouraged us to save all kinds of natural materials from which "critters" could be made.

I still do this collecting, although the creations are a bit more sophisticated by now, and the collection of materials includes large quantities of cloth, yarn, thread, fleece, bark, shells, stones, found feathers, and wood.

17

CHILDREN AND NATURE

THE WAYS that children see the adults in their lives relating to nature will very likely become unquestioned assumptions that will help to shape their own lives. *Last Child in the Woods: Saving Our Children from Nature-Deficit Disorder* by Richard Louv chronicles our society's alienation from nature and the restorative value of reconnecting, including potential help for attention deficit disorder and other dysfunctions. Joseph Chilton Pearce has pointed out in *Evolution's End* and *The Death of Religion and the Rebirth of Spirit* how our television and virtual reality culture is causing neurological changes in children to their detriment. Children need nature.

As populations continue to grow, wild space shrinks, and some city children are dependent on parks and occasional trips for even glimpses of the wild world. Rachel Carson's *The Sense of Wonder* is a timeless reminder of the value of taking children to wild places so that they may become aware of the astonishing variety of life around us. A child benefits from having an adult to share in the discovery of the mystery and beauty of the natural world.

Joseph Cornell's *Sharing Nature with Children* and *Sharing the Joy of Nature* suggest nature activities for all ages. Gardens, even windowsill gardens, bird feeders, and pets allow some daily contact with nature for even city children, but it is how all these are viewed and treated that makes all the difference. Adults must show the way.

Here in Vermont we are fortunate still to have easy access to woods, fields, lakes, and streams, and a child who grows

Children and Nature

up in such an environment is blessed. But it depends on the adults to instill in the child a sense of wonder and an attitude of care for the natural world.

Dorian McGowan and his wife Kari made a seamless world of nature and art for their children and later for visiting grandchildren. Whether teaching art or working at home, Dorian is always "at play," making art or gardens. Everyone in the family is an artist and a lover of nature because art and nature have surrounded them throughout their lives. The family home is on a dirt road and near a stream, in which they all have played, and which has been diverted into little pools that are homes for fish and frogs, water lilies and sculptures. Artwork from the whole family has transformed their home, inside and out, and a new project or a new garden, depending on the season, seemed always underway.

The award-winning artist Mary Azarian also has always combined art and gardens, and her lush and beautiful gardens and the creatures of her country life often have appeared in her woodblock prints and book illustrations.

Vermont is a state with an agricultural heritage and many dairy farms. Photographs of the cows at Jack and Anne Lazor's Butterworks Farm showed them as the happiest cows I have ever seen. They were treated with kindness and care, and with homeopathy if ailing. Butterworks yogurt and cream are well known throughout New England, but the Lazors and their family also have grown organically much of their own food and that for the cows. Jack wrote a book on growing grains—*The Organic Grain Grower*. They developed a lifestyle that was as sustainable as possible and have been always gracious about sharing what they have learned.

There are many other farmers who care deeply for their animals and for their land, but there is distressing omission on some farms of any apparent awareness of the animals or plants on which they depend. Every living thing is holy, as J. G. Bennett reminded us, so let us bless the lives that are given up to give us food and never forget that gift when we prepare the food and are nourished.

Hunting has its own mystique in Vermont as in many places, and compared to the horror of much factory farming, hunting may seem preferable in that the animals and birds live free until death, which can be quick if the hunter is a good shot. But the freedom of wild lives is not without care, for with increasing human population the space and food supplies for wildlife are ever shrinking. And as creatures lose their habitat, where are they to go? I do not feel that wildlife belongs to human beings or that the state can own or should manage wildlife on behalf of the people except in the way of protection for the wildlife. Wild creatures have as much right as people do to live here, and if our numbers are intruding on their space, spoiling their habitat and way of life, it is our responsibility to try to do what we can to right that wrong. Those who "own" land might want to plant what will provide wildlife with food and nesting possibilities and allow creatures space to live unharmed, and to share these thoughts of responsibility and care giving with their children.

It is still an unquestioned assumption for most people that they must have meat to live, even though it has been shown through countless books and personal examples that this is not so and that not only are food resources much more available to others around the world but health is improved for most people when they stop or drastically decrease their eating of meat.

It is interesting but not surprising that many formerly avid hunters come in time to think differently than they once did and eventually no longer wish to kill anything, although they may still enjoy the camaraderie of friends in the woods. If meat eaters hunt, I hope it is with the respect for their prey felt by many so-called primitive people and that they teach this to their children if they expect them to be hunters too. I feel always saddened at the newspaper pictures of young children posed happily with dead bear cubs as their first victims. What is the mindset that says that this is a good thing?

In the spring of 2021 John Robbins and his son Ocean offered a free Food Revolution Summit on the internet. The many excellent speakers, most of them doctors with longtime credentials and many publications, were interviewed by John Robbins, as they, with much recently learned scientific detail, expressed the critical need for human beings to turn to a plant-based diet, as they feel that nature (by our teeth and physical being) intended us to do. Science has now learned that many of our most dreaded chronic diseases are strongly related to what most of us currently eat—and that when people move away from an animal-based diet and instead change to a plant-based diet, many of these diseases will just go away. Also on a plant-based diet people naturally and without effort lose weight if that is needed.

Much about nutrition still is not taught in many allopathic medical schools, and many doctors are thus almost entirely unaware of the effect of our food choices, but those speaking on the Summit are aware and have given a great gift to the public in making this information more widely known. Not only could implementing their suggestions reduce a great amount of human suffering and death, as well as the enormous suffering of the huge number of animals now raised for food, but it also would work toward reducing food inequality and starvation around the world since, instead of the vast amounts of grain now being raised to feed the food animals, food for people could be grown. And it would have a large effect in helping to ease climate change by reducing the energy drain as well as the damage to land, water supplies, and rain forests essential to the planet's well-being that are caused as part of current factory farming and other large-scale food-producing enterprises for feeding the animals raised for food. This is really critical information that needs to be learned and heeded by human beings throughout the world, and it is wonderful that the work that John Robbins began in 1987 with his *Diet for a New America*—and continued with *The Food Revolution* and earlier Summits—has resulted in this very timely recent Summit. If the suggestions made through this Summit could be widely heeded that would certainly be a great gift to the future of the world's children.

18

The Garden

If you want to be happy for a week, take a wife.
If you want to be happy all your life, make a garden.
—Chinese proverb

GARDENS HAVE become an art form, and there are a great many books showing medieval, colonial, English cottage, wildflower, herb, salad, dyeing, water, Oriental, Japanese, sanctuary, and many other kinds of gardens for those who want to create, recreate, or just appreciate them. Feng shui is briefly mentioned in the earth energies chapter, and feng shui in the garden is also now a popular subject matter.

The history of the garden is cobbled together from bits and pieces—vegetable matter found in tombs, ancient artwork, old written accounts, attempts to trace the history of particular plants, and speculation.

Hunter-gatherers roamed seasonally for a long time in human history. Later, farming resulted in more sedentary lives, and what lay beyond the clusters of human habitation became thought of as filled with dangers, so that nature, understood then as wilderness, came for a time to be perceived as enemy. When crops were planted, they needed to be protected. Walled gardens in the west, probably first in the Mediterranean basin, according to Penelope Hobhouse in *Gardening through the Ages*, offered protection from marauders and harsh winds. When walled gardens were created for pleasure, many were also meant to be reminders of paradise.

The Garden

As all natural things may be considered as signs of God, the paradise garden is both sign and reminder. The word *paradise* comes from the Persian word for "walled garden."

In traditional Persian gardens there was usually a *chabutra*, a stone or marble platform, later perhaps with a pavilion or garden tent or sometimes a miniature mountain at the center. This kind of paradise garden included a cross of water, reminiscent of the four rivers of paradise—water, milk, honey, and wine—meeting at the central, the omphalos point, and so dividing the garden into four parts, the *chahar bagh*, representing the world. In desert countries water was very special and it flowed from the mountains in *qanats*, tunnels dug with air holes at intervals for air for the workers who dug the tunnels. Near the village, water was apportioned, and rights to it were purchased, so having water in the garden was a rare treat, and it was honored as representing the Water of Life.

Traditionally, according to Julia Berrall in *The Garden*, in every Persian garden were four essentials: water for irrigation and serenity; shade for coolness and shelter; flowers for color and fragrance; and music. Tenth century stories of the gardens of caliphs of Baghdad told of a gold and silver tree in which gold and silver birds whistled.

Henry Corbin comments on the motif of the garden in Persian painting, noting that where there is the lack of classical perspective, all elements are represented in the present. The viewer is meant to give attention to each of the elements in a mental itinerary, so that the picture functions as a mandala for contemplation. Corbin says that this is "the 'perspective' by which the disciple of Khidr orients himself, and which permits him, through the symbolic rite of circumambulation, to attain to the 'center of the world.'"[1]

In Persian paintings sometimes there are people sitting in the pavilion, and the idea there is similar to that in a Japanese tea garden. One sat in the pavilion and observed what was around one. The blossoming plum or almond signified life and hope; the cypress, immortality.

The ancient Persians had a secret language of flowers, according to Henry Corbin in *Spiritual Body and Celestial Earth*. What was planted in the gardens had very specific spiritual associations, although I still have not been able to discover more than hints about the precise meanings for individual plants.

In *Journeys with a Sufi Master* H. B. M. Dervish says that he was told that the aesthetic value and active chemical curative substances flowers contain are not what is most important about them, but that there are advantages in growing certain kinds of flowers that correspond with environmental factors, although this was not explained. Nasturtiums, blue poppies, dwarf willow, and cress were highly prized. The cardamom seed was said to be full of *baraka* (blessing); the pine kernel nut was food of wisdom; saffron was food of health; rice with spices, the food of life.

An idea that comes from the Mazdean (Zoroastrian) tradition is that each flower represents a different angel, and as you contemplate a particular flower you call upon that angel. This is similar to the contemporary idea of meditating on a plant and having the deva speak to you, as described in the Findhorn and Perelandra books.

A Persian dwelling of the past had few furnishings, mainly a carpet and pillows for sitting on the floor. For winter the garden was brought inside in the form of the garden carpet, which often showed the fourfold pattern intersected by water. The intent in both paradise garden and carpet was to direct the mind toward paradise.

In a medieval Christian parchment showing monks climbing to heaven, one is seen reaching out to either smell or pluck a flower and falling off the ladder. According to that code, he was apparently getting too sensually involved with nature.

However, among medieval Christian gardens, one kind was called the Mary garden. In a Mary garden everything had meaning. Berrall describes how in a Rhenish painting of the fifteenth century the enclosed garden itself symbolizes the virgin birth. The iris has a regal connotation. Mary's purity is suggested by the white lilies, divine love by the red roses. The cherry tree suggests the joys of heaven. Strawberries are the fruits of righteousness, with leaves symbolizing the Trinity. On the table are apples, reminiscent of humanity's fall and redemption by Christ. The water trough associates Mary with "the well of living waters," and lilies of the valley denote her meekness. Goldfinches on the wall are associated with the Passion, for they have crimson markings and eat seeds of the thorny thistle.

Often in Mary gardens were roses, for the rose represented the female connected with the earth, purity, and divine love.

The rose, which was also very important in Persian gardens, has been an important symbol in the Sufi tradition, used by many writers but thought of now especially in connection with Rumi and the Mevlevi Sufis.

In the Islamic tradition there seems to be a distinction made between paradise and the imaginal world, with paradise only to be entered at the end of time. But Hurqalya seems to be understood as what some would consider to be a paradise. The idea in some of the ancient Sufi writings, as I understand it, is that one journeys after death to ever subtler realms, at each phase of the journey leaving behind a body that is denser and receiving one of finer quality.

In the Sufi tradition Hurqalya, the imaginal world, is thought of as the intermediate world that surrounds this world and that is entered from the cosmic mountain Qaf, at the top of which is the emerald stone. This world of Hurqalya

The Garden

is green but invisible to ordinary physical sight, although it is said that it is what makes the sky appear blue. The access to this world while we are alive is the imagination, which does not mean fantasy. Henry Corbin's books go into this in detail.

Everything in our mundane world mirrors what is above in the real reality. In this tradition it is as though you are in the bottom of a well, climbing up, for all meaning comes from above. Those from this Sufi tradition are interested in subtle cosmology, for that is what is real, while all the rest is illusion. You will remember that the meaning from above is understood to be from the "orient." The "occident" is down here, this world of forms, subject to all the misinterpretations of the senses.

In this tradition, part of the task of a human being in our world is to bring into being the essential body, the subtle body with its more subtle senses, that will allow the person to experience Hurqalya after death, although some may become able to experience Hurqalya while still alive. In Hurqalya you may speak with trees and rocks and everything else. (Some of us may learn how to do that here as well!)

In *Spiritual Body and Celestial Earth*, Henry Corbin quotes the idea that the essential body of the faithful believer is "fashioned according to the extent of his knowledge, to his capacity to understand, to his spiritual consciousness, to his moral conduct."[2] The more subtle the body becomes, the greater its magnitude, so that the size of the paradise of the faithful adept is measured by those qualities. One may have an essential body seven, ten, a million times greater than this terrestrial world. Each creates a dwelling place in proportion to the capacity of his or her spiritual energy. Nobody can escape from her- or himself or become other than that. The essential or archetypal body becomes itself his or her paradise.

What this means is that your thought, your consciousness, is what you become after death, and the paradise garden and the paradise garden carpet constantly remind you of this.

Hazrat Inayat Khan said that we create the world we go to "as a spider lives in the web it has woven."[3]

Robert Lawlor's *Voices of the First Day*, about the worldview of the Australian Aboriginals, perhaps the oldest civilization on earth, describes the easy back and forth passage in consciousness that seems to be made by these people between their everyday world and the dreamtime. These two different realms seem to me to suggest what David Bohm meant by secondary and primary reality. And the easy accessing of the primary realm also seems similar to what is happening in Robert Wolff's *Original Wisdom*, and also what it means to go in consciousness to Shambhala or to Hurqalya. Henry Corbin makes it very clear that Hurqalya is a real place, although one not experienced through our ordinary senses. Suprasensory senses are required, a different mindset that must be learned or achieved or received before access may be had. Hurqalya is a realm to which we may move after death, but it is a place that we potentially may learn to visit while still alive. Consciousness is the vehicle. At least this is my understanding.

There were many other than liturgical kinds of gardens created over the years, but for the most part these also were enclosed spaces, set aside for a particular purpose. According to Paul Shepard in *Man in the Landscape*, it was not until the walls of gardens started to come down at the end of the seventeenth and in the eighteenth century that all of nature began to be viewed as a garden, and this is when contemporary ideas of nature, landscape, and tourism began.

Gardens are widespread today. As reaction to the chemical fertilizer emphasis of recent times, organic farming and gardening slowly have been gaining wider acceptance. Biodynamic gardening is practiced in many places. Books by John Seymour (*The Self-Sufficient Gardener*) and Eliot Coleman (*The New Organic Grower, Four-Season Harvest, The Winter Harvest Handbook*) have guided us in our efforts. In *Gaia's*

The Garden

Garden: A Guide to Home-Scale Permaculture, Toby Hemenway introduces plans for an ecological and permaculture garden—an exciting concept toward which to move and especially interesting in that it emulates the way nature works when left alone. The idea is to grow not single crops but many different ones together, making them less insect-prone and able to support each other with their diversity. Fruit trees are grown with crops underneath them, and the homestead gradually becomes self-sufficient, but in a more natural looking way than gardens have looked before. As we all need to become more self-sufficient, permaculture seems a prime gardening method to investigate. Rosalind Creasy's updated *Edible Landscape* suggests a delightful and nourishing alternative to lawns.

After studying the meanings that have accrued to plants in various traditions, you may decide to make a part of or one of your own gardens a personal contemplative one. In *Sacred Flowers: Creating a Heavenly Garden*, Roni Jay refers to the daisy as belonging to the sun, with a daisy chain joined at the ends representing the sun and the total world it sustains. The five-petalled rose, she says, represents Christ on earth, divine love in earthly form, but she also gives the sacred meaning of the rose in other traditions. So if you choose to have a daisy or a rose be part of your garden, you may now have many associations in mind, for once you are aware of the folklore, historical, geometrical, or numerical associations of plants and trees, their meaning to you will surely be enlarged, and you will want to treat them with new respect and care.

You will want to make gardens welcoming to wildlife as well, for knowing more about wild creatures must change or enhance your relationship with them. You may want to connect with the nature intelligences as has been done by individuals and at Findhorn and Perelandra. You may learn to communicate with insects and animals you formerly considered pests and make agreements with them as Machaelle Small Wright did, leaving some plants for the wild brethren but asking that they leave the rest for you. If you are sincere, you may be amazed at what happens after such requests. You may find dowsing a helpful tool in the garden. Herbalist Adele Dawson, author of *Herbs: Partners in Life,* dowsed and found a place in her northern Vermont garden where a fragile plant from the Southwest could thrive.

In *Secret Teachings in the Art of Japanese Gardens* David A. Slawson describes a reprimand given to him when, as an apprentice, he was squatting with both feet flat on the ground and sweeping between plants in a tea garden in Kyoto. Fatigued, he shifted his weight onto the ball of his left foot, but he was rebuked and told to imagine a garden master who was blind and who sensed the uneven distribution of his weight causing a disturbance in the atmosphere of the garden. Every action in the garden, he was told, must be done in the spirit of harmony the garden was meant to convey. The conscious awareness with which the work is done does make a difference in any kind of garden or activity.

Japanese gardens are a very beautiful and diverse art form, whether they are large viewing gardens or small spaces associated with the tea ceremony or are bonsai trees in pots. For contemplation, moss gardens and stone gardens—raked sand or gravel and boulders such as in the famous Ryōanji stone garden in Kyoto—are other versions of the disciplined beauty associated with this tradition and indicative of great respect for nature, not only for the growing plants but also for the contributions of the mineral kingdom.

Awareness of your garden space may be your first real connection with nature, and a great deal can be realized within even a small area. If you do not have a garden space of your own, investigate having a share in one of the many community gardens now springing up across the country.

The Garden

A TV special on Philadelphia gardens told how they had become showcases for artwork as well as for growing food. The Village of Arts and Humanities in Philadelphia, the inspiration of Lily Yeh, is profiled in Elizabeth Murray's *Cultivating Sacred Space: Gardening for the Soul*. It began with one empty lot and over ten years fifty-five abandoned properties were turned into "parks, gardens, educational facilities, offices, and low-income housing. This has made the Village an oasis of trees, flowers, murals and brightly colored mosaics and has enriched the lives of hundreds of children, unemployed adults and anyone else the project touches."[4] Lily Yeh, an Asian woman, an outsider coming to this trash-strewn ghetto neighborhood, was given an empty lot for an artistic statement in 1985. She said she didn't know how to start, but began with a circle in the center. Her work was to "transform the neighborhood and through that we build people and we heal from the bottom up. . . . So from nothing we can make wonderful things, and that's what we want to teach our children."[5]

Plants on windowsills and in window boxes or pots bring beauty to small spaces and have lessons to teach. And an increasing number of people have become interested in bonsai culture. This tradition from China and Japan results in the miniaturization of trees that may be hundreds of years old. Sometimes people feel that training bonsai means imposing an outside will upon the trees, but ideally it means finding out from the trees what they wish to become and how this is to be accomplished.

The localvore way of eating is coming to attention now as farmers' markets and CSAs (community sustained agriculture) or other farm-to-family shares are becoming more popular. The consumer develops a relationship with the grower and can be assured that organic methods have been used in the production of the food.

The Chinese proverb with which this section began closes with "If you want to be happy all your life, make a garden."

Gratitude is a major subject in Robin Wall Kimmerer's *Braiding Sweetgrass*. Her book is filled with recognition of all that is given to us through the earth and the earth's various kingdoms. As a biologist, there is much detail in the book about what the plant world offers—everything that we need!

What a great debt of gratitude we owe to the plant kingdom for sustaining us—and for so much enjoyment and so many lessons along the way.

19

The Green Man

PAN WAS mentioned in connection with the Findhorn garden. Pan also has a presence in literature, and many will recall his fleeting appearance in *The Wind in the Willows*.

Pan is related to the concept of the Green Man, which has a long history, including the idea of the wild man from the wilderness. The Green Man image appeared throughout Europe in the Middle Ages and is represented in Gothic cathedrals, often as leaf-framed faces peering out at the tops of columns that were originally meant to symbolize trees. The Green Man appears in various guises in folk festivals and is still seen in wood or stone carvings in old Christian churches in Great Britain and on the Continent. In *The Green Man: The Archetype of Our Oneness with the Earth* William Anderson says that this figure "symbolizes the union of humanity and the vegetable world. He knows and utters the secret laws of Nature."[1] Resurgence of interest in this figure of exuberant life seems significant now, and there are many contemporary treatments of this theme in the art world. John Fowles says in *The Tree* that "There is something in the nature of nature, in its presentness, its seeming transience, its creative ferment and hidden potential, that corresponds very closely with the wild, or green man, in our psyches."[2]

There are other figures that express this sense of timeless life. Utnapishtim, for whom Gilgamesh went in search, is such a figure. There are stories of Alexander the Great going in search of the Water of Life with his cook Andreas: when a few drops of water splash accidentally on a cooked fish, it revives and swims away, and they know then that they have found the place they sought. There is a similar story about Khidr.

Khidr, like Elijah, is considered to be an immortal, one who does not die. A number of paintings show Elijah and Khidr at the spring that represents the Water of Life. It is where the two worlds meet or "where the two seas meet"—this world and the world beyond. Sometimes Khidr is described as living in rivers and riding a fish, but usually he is said to live on a green island marked by a rock in the sea.

Khidr is described as a friend of God and one who knows and does God's will. There are stories of Khidr and Moses, where Moses begs to go with Khidr and Khidr tells him that he will not have the patience to observe but not question what Khidr does. And what Khidr said is exactly what happens, for each time that Khidr performs an action that seems wrong, Moses is upset and asks him to explain. Khidr sinks a boat—to save it from pirates. He helps to build up a wall to hide a treasure—until the rightful young owners will be old enough to find and take charge of it themselves. An evil young man is killed—Khidr knowing that his parents will have a worthier son. In each case, although the action Khidr takes appalls Moses, who does not know the inner meaning of it, Khidr was doing God's will and so what was appropriate. Moses did not have the "patience" to wait to understand. These are vivid lessons in the limitations of our earthly judgments.

Khidr is considered to be the special friend of the Sufi and the one who will lead one out of the desert if he is called upon. The cloak of Khidr is granted to special beings like Ibn 'Arabi. The saying "to put on the sandals of Khidr" means to experience through his special being, and one can aspire to know the "Khidr" of one's own being. Khidr wears green and can bring a cooked fish back to life so that it swims away. Sara

Sviri's chapter on Khidr in *The Taste of Hidden Things* is a fine introduction to this special being, of whom she says,

> Khidr is believed to be walking on the skin of the earth, and wherever he steps green shoots come forth. His touch and presence bring things to life. He is endowed with the power of finding water which is hidden in the depth of the earth. He can be present in many places at one and the same time. He materializes in many disguises and forms. He is the one who appears in desperate situations to the "constrained" . . . and removes all obstacles.[3]

Khidr is the quintessential Green Man. He is also, according to Victoria LePage in *Shambhala*, the prototype of the Shambhalic Guardian. She mentions that René Guénon refers to Shambhala-Agarttha (Agarttha being the underground storehouse of the world's wisdom) as an organization through which immortals like Khidr communicate sacred wisdom of nonhuman origin to those with the capacity to receive it.

20

THE MIRROR AND TRANSPARENCY

SOME OF our personal sense of self comes from the mirror. *In Coming to Our Senses*, Morris Berman wrote about the development and use of the mirror as accompanying periods of self-awareness. From this self-awareness, however, unfortunately can come a division of the once seamless world into a split between "I" and what becomes thought of as "it," a division that causes much misunderstanding and strife.

In the Sufi tradition there is an entirely different understanding of the mirror. One is urged to polish the mirror of the heart (a saying that comes from a time when mirrors were made of metal) so that it will better reflect the Divine. Where the mirror is turned and how well it is polished make all the difference.

If one does succeed in mirroring at least something of the Divine, all nature seems to reflect that change in consciousness. We think at once of the animals and birds flocking around Saint Francis.

In *Man and Nature* Seyyed Hossein Nasr says that "Man sees in nature what he is himself. . . . Men who live only on the surface of their being can study nature as something to be manipulated and dominated. But only he who has turned toward the inward dimension of his being can see nature as a symbol, as a transparent reality and come to know and understand it in a real sense."[1]

Part of understanding the transparency of nature is recognizing that reality is multileveled, with many veils that can both hide and reveal—but that all are part of a greater Unity.

The Mirror and Transparency

One may desire to become so transparent—so un-dense, so unlimited by the ego (or with the sense of the ego so expanded that it includes all)—that one can recognize that what is without is also within, and the reverse. The understanding is that behind all multiplicity is a Unity and that, while enjoying and participating in the multiplicity, we want to remember what truly connects—the Oneness that includes all. How do we learn to penetrate or lift some of the veils? Some ways are through symbol, story, awareness of the imaginal world and dreamtime, investing the landscape here with qualities of the imaginal world, the personification of the landscape—the understanding of the "angel" of the landscape, awareness of the shamanic vision, folklore meanings and associations, awareness of geomancy and the earth currents, of geometry and pattern, and by efforts to enter the consciousness of other beings and to relate to them in new ways. These are some of the doors that, if opened, may offer new vistas and fresh ways to begin to see.

But it does seem that we have to be taught to see. As a young person, after reading Arthur Conan Doyle's Sherlock Holmes books, I made great efforts to not just look but really to "see." Paul Shepherd's *Man in the Landscape* tells how people in the eighteenth century learned to "see" landscape by facing the other way and holding up a Claude glass, a darkened and framed convex mirror that "framed" the view. I think of stories of natives unable to see Captain Cook's ship, invisible to them because they had never before seen such a thing. And of Reshad Feild, identifying a single rare shell on a beach where he had noticed none before and then suddenly seeing them everywhere. It seems that we have to know something about something or in some way have our attention directed to it in order for recognition to take place.

Through its beauty, its intricacy, and its mystery nature reveals to us, to the extent that we have the capacity to understand, as much as we can know of the Divine, the sum of all that is.

In *What Is God?* Jacob Needleman details his life's efforts to answer the question of his title. In the course of the book a further question becomes what is the human being? Much of his answer came to him through study of Gurdjieff's teachings. He responds to the frequent question about how can there be a God conceived of as good when there is so much misery in the world by saying

> how could the human race have ever dreamt that God could act in a merciful, just manner in the human world without the presence of individual men and women who have received the inward God of consciousness within their own human frame? This is the real unrecognized illusion about religion in our world . . . that God can and should act mercifully and justly in human history without the "instrument" of God-inhabited human beings.[2]

The creation of that human instrument, the bringing forth into manifestation of the latent possibility of the perfected human being is what is intended through spiritual teaching and practice. All of our hands then may become the "hands of God." The internal question then is: How can these hands and hearts best serve?

21

THE HEART

THE HEART has a very important role in our relating to and understanding "nature's manuscript." First of all we can understand this as meaning the opening of the heart, the development of compassion.

In *The Prophet's Way* Thom Hartmann tells of looking out the window and seeing his German teacher, Herr Müller, picking up worms on the wet road and carrying them to safety—this done quietly, without an audience. As a step toward bettering our world this is a suggestion Hartmann passes along: do small acts of compassion in secret (in other words, not for the ego effect). A similar tale of rescuing worms is told of Saint Francis. And there are also small creature rescue scenes in the writing of Joseph Bruchac (in "Birdfoot's Grandpa" in *Entering Onondaga*) and Jan de Hartog (in *The Centurion*), describing the carrying to safety of toads that cross busy highways in New York State and in England in the spring.

Compassion is the touchstone of what is taught in many traditions. When one thinks of the Buddha or of Kwan Yin or of the Dalai Lama, that is the first teaching that comes to mind.

To understand still more about the heart, Henry Corbin reminds us that in Ibn 'Arabi and Sufism "the heart . . . is the organ which produces true knowledge, comprehensive intuition, and gnosis . . . of God and the divine mysteries, in short, the organ of everything connoted by the term 'esoteric science.'"[1] Corbin also refers to the heart as the "eye" through which God knows Himself. William Chittick, writing about Rumi, says, "The ultimate center of man's consciousness, his inmost reality, his 'meaning' as known by God, is called the 'heart.'"[2] Rumi, in a Coleman Barks version, calls this kind of knowing "A freshness in the center of the chest."[3]

This "freshness in the center of the chest," this spring, is the intelligence of the heart, which may also be understood as finely tuned intuition. It is from this source that your most accurate knowing comes. As Hazrat Inayat Khan said, "The heart is the gate of God; as soon as you knock upon it, the answer comes."[4] The subtle heart connects us with the universe beyond our physical selves.

In *The Way to Shambhala*, Edwin Bernbaum wrote of the eight-petalled lotus that symbolizes the heart center or wheel of truth: "Certain lamas . . . identify the inner Shambhala with this center and point out that the highest or innermost mind, the only one capable of knowing the true nature of reality, is supposed to be hidden there."[5] Later he wrote that "the eight petal-shaped regions of Shambhala stand for eight psychic nerves or channels that are supposed to radiate out like spokes of a wheel from the center of the heart. These nerves then divide and subdivide into thousands of threadlike branches that fan out, in turn, to the various sense organs and mental faculties of the body."[6]

The Hindu *Upanishads* say that the divine "Self, who understands all, and whose glory is manifest in the universe, lives within the lotus of the heart."[7]

In ancient Egypt, according to Robert Lawlor in *Sacred Geometry*, the achievement of that quality of understanding called the "intelligence of the heart" was life's goal.

In *The HeartMath Solution* Doc Childre and Howard Martin say that Mesopotamians, Egyptians, Babylonians, and Greeks felt that the primary organ capable of directing energies and decisions is the heart. In ancient Judaic tradition the heart is the center of beauty, harmony, and balance. Balance is related to the heart in yogic traditions, and the physical heart is thought of as the internal guru. In Chinese medicine the heart is seen as the connection between mind and body.

In *Evolution's End* Joseph Chilton Pearce wrote of the third stage of human development as the "highest heart." He said, "Two poles of experience lie within us, our unique, individual self generating through the brain; and a universal, impersonal intelligence generating through the heart. . . . Unfortunately," he wrote at that time, "no academic concept or nurturing model-environment is provided for a 'heart's intelligence,' making our ignorance of it a dismal and crippling fact."[8] Later he referred to love not as a sentiment but as a power, "that intelligence of the heart that moves for our overall well-being."[9] His teacher told him that the intelligence of the heart did not solve problems but dissolved the situations in which problems exist. His teacher also said that one must develop the intellect to become a proper instrument for the intelligence of the heart, but that only the heart can develop the intellect to its highest extent.

The idea of the intelligence of the heart, as you can see from the examples given, is certainly not new, but we seem to keep forgetting about this and so have to begin all over again.

Pearce pointed out in *The Death of Religion and the Rebirth of Spirit* that Rudolf Steiner predicted that the "greatest discovery of late-twentieth century science would be that the heart is not merely a pump but also a major source of intelligence" and that our challenge would be to "allow the heart to teach us a new way to think, which, it seems, would open us to higher worlds."[10]

The HeartMath Institute came into being to scientifically study this idea of the intelligence of the heart and has done studies that show that the heart responds to information before the brain does, that the heart intuits and responds to information before it is even processed and decided upon by a random generator. Heart awareness is understood to be in essence intuition. The heart directs and aligns many systems in the body so that they can function harmoniously together, has its own nervous system, and signals from the heart to the brain affect "areas and functions in the amygdala, the thalamus, and the cortex."[11]

In the Sufi tradition there are rare beings known as "Possessors of the Heart," finely attuned to the Divine through intuition.

Henry Corbin says, "To possess the science of the heart is to perceive the divine metamorphoses, that is to say, the multiplicity and the transformation of the forms. . . . Thus it is to know the Divine Being through intuitive vision, to perceive Him in the form in which each of his epiphanies shows itself."[12] Dogmatists can never convince each other, but by disclosing its limit, the science of the heart transmutes dogma.

In *The Reflective Heart* James Morris wrote about those who recognize the Divine only in the form they have come to expect. Ibn 'Arabi wrote what the Divine thinks of that: "whoever restricts Me to one form rather than another is really only worshiping what they themselves have imagined."[13] And so when Ibn 'Arabi writes, "My heart has become capable of every form," he means that he can see the Divine within whatever forms and whatever religious trappings are used.

To come back to contemporary thinking, in *The Secret Teachings of Plants* Stephen Harrod Buhner recognizes the heart, not as had long been thought, the pump that moves the blood along (for he says that blood apparently moves on its own), but as the vital organ of perception and communication, responsive to influences from within and without, and regulating blood flow accordingly. Buhner reports that a too-regular heartbeat can be a sign of illness and stresses the need for heart/brain coherence that develops from heart-centered cognition rather than just mind intelligence. We have not been trained in our society to understand our heart function in this way. Buhner says,

> Redeveloping the capacity for heart-centered cognition can help each of us reclaim personal perception of the living and sacred intelligence within the world, within each particular thing. It moves us from a rational orientation in a dead, mechanized universe to one in which the unique perceptions of the heart are noticed and strengthened, to a deep experience of the living soulfulness of the world. As the process continues to deepen, it strengthens our spiritual sensitivity and ... helps us gain a deeper understanding of our own sacredness.[14]

Developing heart-centered cognition requires the unfolding of awareness of other ways of knowing, as has been stressed throughout this book. These ways are related to the ways in which a shaman functions. In *The Dream of the Earth* Thomas Berry wrote that

> This shamanic insight is especially important just now when history is being made ... between humans and the earth, with all its living creatures. In this context all our professions and institutions must be judged primarily by the extent to which they foster this mutually enhancing human-earth relationship.
>
> If the supreme disaster in the comprehensive story of the earth is our present closing down of the major life systems of the planet, then the supreme need of our times is to bring about a healing of the earth through this mutually enhancing presence to the earth community.... [A] new type of sensitivity is needed, a sensitivity that is something more than romantic attachment to some of the more brilliant manifestations of the natural world, a sensitivity that comprehends the larger patterns of nature, its severe demands as well as its delightful aspects, and is willing to see the human diminish so that other lifeforms might flourish.[15]

In his essay in *Thomas Berry: Dreamer of the Earth* Matthew Fox picks up on this theme of the need for the shamanic personality, saying that Berry was calling us to "the 'numinous' relationship with the cosmos, that is our birthright and is also our way back to our own healing, our own instincts, our own *ground*." [16]

The kind of relationship to the cosmos that Berry and Fox are referring to as shamanic is also the way of the dowser and of the spiritual seeker who recognizes the interconnection of all that is and our human responsibility to express our awareness of that interconnection with heart intelligence and love in all that we do.

If heart intelligence and this relationship to nature were to be implemented by even a few to begin, and by morphic resonance could reach the 100th monkey stage where this Opening of the Way would spread, imagine what a difference there could be.

22

Bringing it All Together

I HOPE THAT this slim volume, pointing toward some of what has interested me, will catch your fancy enough to get you thinking and reading and practicing in some of the directions suggested. Once you begin, you will probably find, as I have, that byway leads to byway and that there is always more to learn.

The sum of it all is that we are deeply blessed to be a part of nature, for in addition to all the sensory pleasures she offers, nature is probably our best textbook and path toward understanding ourselves and the world in which we live. We will never get to the end of that learning, but surely effort and intention will change us and, we trust, help us to become more of what human beings are intended to be.

Attention and true listening are necessary on this path, and perhaps they are the best definition of prayer. In *Natural Prayers* Chet Raymo wrote, "Learning to pray, then, as I understand it, is learning to listen with the mind and heart—making oneself *attentive* to each exquisite detail of the world."[1] In her poem "Messenger," Mary Oliver says, "My work is loving the world ... which is mostly standing still and learning to be astonished."[2]

As we become more and more aware of the beauty and the complexity that are in all of creation, gratitude fills our hearts that we are able both to witness and to be part of it all, this multiple expression on earth of the Divine. Human wonder, gratitude, and love are very important, for it is the passion of our caring that will change our lives and, as we learn to express the love of creation through our beings, aid in that awakening in others. And creation will respond: as you take ten steps toward it, it will take ten toward you.

Animals, birds, trees, plants, and all other aspects of nature have wisdom to share and will respond to your caring attention. The more you realize the interconnection of all that is, the more you are able to expand your ability to move beyond limitations of the small ego self. A corollary of that expansion is the realization that you are able to communicate with what you once thought of as "other" but now know is really part of yourself. When you become aware of this, you will be amazed at what you can learn.

For all of us, may the "eye of the soul" be opened so that we may each day understand more of nature's manuscript. The lessons are there, waiting for us.

Notes

Foreword

1. Nancy Wilson Ross, *Buddhism: A Way of Life and Thought* (New York: Random House, 1981), 55.

2. John Broomfield, *Other Ways of Knowing: Recharting Our Future with Ageless Wisdom* (Rochester, VT: Inner Traditions International, 1997), 1.

3. Seyyed Hossein Nasr, *Man and Nature: The Spiritual Crisis of Modern Man* (London: Unwin Hyman Limited, 1990), 14.

4. Ibid., 21.

5. Ibid., 132.

Introduction

1. Chet Raymo, *When God Is Gone Everything Is Holy* (Notre Dame, IN: Sorin Books, 2008), 22.

2. Ibid., 140.

Chapter 1: Other Ways of Knowing

1. Arthur Deikman, quoted by Frances E. Vaughan in *Awakening Intuition* (Garden City, New York: Anchor Press, 1979), 178.

2. Joseph Chilton Pearce, *The Death of Religion and the Rebirth of Spirit: A Return to the Intelligence of the Heart* (Rochester, VT: Park Street Press, 2007), 178–79.

3. Ibid., 180.

4. Hans Peter Duerr, *Dreamtime: Concerning the Boundary between Wilderness and Civilization*, translated by Felicitas Goodman (Oxford and New York: Basil Blackwell, 1985), 115.

5. Coleman Barks with John Moyne et al., *A Year with Rumi: Daily Readings* (New York: HarperCollins, 2006), 43.

Notes

Chapter 2: Science, Geometry, Pattern and Proportion, Encoding, and More

1. Massimo Citro, MD, *The Basic Code of the Universe: The Science of the Invisible in Physics, Medicine, and Spirituality* (Rochester, VT: Park Street Press, 2011), 6–8.

2. György Doczi, *The Power of Limits: Proportional Harmonies in Nature, Art, and Architecture* (Boulder, CO: Shambhala, 1981), 1.

3. Ibid., 7.

4. Ibid., 1.

5. Nader Ardalan and Laleh Bakhtiar, *The Sense of Unity: The Sufi Tradition in Persian Architecture* (Chicago and London: The University of Chicago Press, 1973), 24.

6. Robert Lawlor, *Sacred Geometry* (London/New York: Thames and Hudson/Crossroad, 1982), 56.

7. Ibid., 4.

8. Ibid.

9. Ibid., 4-5.

10. John Michell with Allan Brown, *How the World Is Made: The Story of Creation According to Sacred Geometry* (Rochester, VT: Inner Traditions, 2009), 6.

11. Ibid., 2.

12. Nigel Pennick, *Sacred Geometry: Symbolism and Purpose in Religious Structures* (San Francisco: Harper & Row, 1982), 7.

13. Idries Shah, *The Sufis* (Garden City, NY: Anchor Books, 1971), 198–99.

14. Preface by Jeff Berkowitz in *Fractal Cosmos: The Art of Mathematical Design* (Oakland, CA: Dharma Enterprises/Amber Lotus, 1994), viii.

15. James Gleick, *Chaos: Making a New Science* (New York: Viking Penguin, 1987), 23.

Chapter 3: The Music of the Spheres

1. David Tame, *The Secret Power of Music: The Transformation of Self and Society through Musical Energy* (Wellingborough, UK: Turnstone Press, 1984), 228.

Notes

2. Ibid.

3. Joachim-Ernst Berendt, *Nada Brahma: The World Is Sound*, translated by Helmut Bredigkeit. (Rochester, VT: Destiny Books, 1987), 77-78.

4. Ibid., 80.

5. Citro, *The Basic Code of the Universe*, 107.

6. Steven Halpern, *Tuning the Human Instrument* (Belmont, CA: Spectrum Research Institute, 1978), 63.

7. Joachim-Ernst Berendt, *The Third Ear: On Listening to the World*, translated by Tim Nevill (New York: Henry Holt & Co., 1985), 101.

8. Peter Tompkins and Christopher Bird, *Secrets of the Soil* (New York: Harper & Row, 1989), 135.

9. Ibid., 136.

Chapter 4: Light

1. Henry Corbin, *The Man of Light in Iranian Sufism*, translated by Nancy Pearson (Boulder, CO: Shambhala Publications, 1978), 111.

2. Citro, *The Basic Code of the Universe*, 182.

3. Peter Russell, *From Science to God: The Mystery of Consciousness and the Meaning of Light* (Las Vegas, NV: Elf Rock Productions, 2002), 90.

4. Rupert Sheldrake in Matthew Fox and Rupert Sheldrake, *The Physics of Angels: Exploring the Realm Where Science and Spirit Meet* (New York: HarperCollins, 1996), 67–69.

5. Ibid., 74.

6. Ibid., 107.

7. Ibid., 135.

8. Richard Gerber, MD, *Vibrational Medicine for the 21st Century: The Complete Guide to Energy Healing and Spiritual Transformation* (New York: HarperCollins, 2000), 219.

9. Jacob Liberman, *Light: Medicine of the Future* (Santa Fe, NM: Bear & Co.,1991), xx.

Chapter 6: Earth Energies

1. Craig F. Stead in a dowsing talk.

2. John Michell, *The Earth Spirit: Its Ways, Shrines, and Mysteries* (New York: Avon Books, 1975), 17.

3. Robin Wall Kimmerer, *Braiding Sweetgrass: Indigenous Wisdom, Scientific Knowledge, and the Teachings of Plants* (Minneapolis, MN: Milkweed Editions, 2013), 384.

Chapter 7: Harmony with the Cosmos

1. Hafiz, "The Sun Never Says," in *Love Poems from God: Twelve Sacred Voices from the East and West,* translated by Daniel Ladinsky (New York: Penguin Compass, 2002), 170.

2. Seyyed Hossein Nasr, *The Garden of Truth: The Vision and Promise of Sufism, Islam's Mystical Tradition* (New York: HarperCollins, 2007), 24.

3. Adrian House, *Francis of Assisi: A Revolutionary Life* (Mahwah, NJ: Hidden Spring/Paulist Press, 2001), 268.

Chapter 9: The World of Plants

1. Peter Tompkins and Christopher Bird, *The Secret Life of Plants* (New York: Harper & Row, 1973), 136.

2. Ibid., 140.

3. The Findhorn Community, *The Findhorn Garden: Pioneering a New Vision of Humanity and Nature in Cooperation* (Forres, Scotland: Findhorn Press, 1988), 112.

4. Ibid.

5. Ibid., 116.

6. Eliot Cowan, *Plant Spirit Medicine* (Newberg, OR: Swan.Raven & Co., 1995), 20.

7. Fred Hageneder, *The Spirit of Trees: Science, Symbiosis, and Inspiration* (New York: Continuum International, 2001), 28.

8. Ibid., 39.

9. Ibid., 47.

10. Roger Cook, *The Tree of Life: Image for the Cosmos* (New York: Avon Books, 1974), 6.

11. Steve Blamires, *Celtic Tree Mysteries: Practical Druid Magic and Divination* (St. Paul, MN: Llewellyn Publications, 2003), 55.

12. Ibid., 216.

13. David Suzuki with Amanda McConnell and Adrienne Mason, *The Sacred Balance: Rediscovering Our Place in Nature*, updated and expanded (Vancouver: Greystone Books, 2007), 32.

Chapter 10: The World of Animals

1. Brian J. Ford, *The Secret Language of Life: How Animals and Plants Feel and Communicate* (New York: Fromm International, 2000), xii.

2. Ibid., xv.

3. David M. Guss, ed., *The Language of the Birds: Tales, Texts, and Poems of Interspecies Communication* (San Francisco: North Point Press, 1985), xi.

4. Joseph Chilton Pearce, *Magical Child Matures* (New York: E. P. Dutton, Inc., 1985), 60.

Chapter 11: Air

1. Ellen Fremedon, *Windforest: Spirit Brooding on Brooding Spirit* (New York: Continuum, 2000), 69.

2. Lyall Watson, *Heaven's Breath: A Natural History of the Wind* (New York: William Morrow & Co., 1984), 7.

3. Ibid., 260.

4. Peter Gold, *Navajo and Tibetan Sacred Wisdom: The Circle of the Spirit* (Rochester, VT: Inner Traditions International, 1994), 188.

Chapter 14: Water

1. Rumi, *We Are Three: New Rumi Poems*, translated by Coleman Barks (Athens, GA: Maypop Books, 1987), 25.

2. Patrick Flanagan and Gael Crystal Flanagan, *Elixir of the Ageless: You Are What You Drink* (Flagstaff, AZ: Vortex Press, 1986), 92.

3. Patricia C. Wright and Richard D. Wright, *The Divining Heart: Dowsing and Spiritual Unfoldment* (Rochester, VT: Destiny Books, 1994), 82.

4. Citro, *The Basic Code of the Universe*, 41.

5. Larry Dossey, MD, *Space, Time and Medicine* (Boulder, CO: Shambhala, 1982), 189.

6. Citro, *The Basic Code of the Universe*, 172.

7. Ibid.

Chapter 15: The World of Fish and Other Water Creatures

1. Amy Corzine, *The Secret Life of the Universe: The Quest for the Soul of Science* (London/New York: Watkins Publishing/Sterling Publishing, 2008), 120.

Chapter 16: Art

1. Titus Burckhardt, *Sacred Art in East and West: Its Principles and Methods,* translated by Lord Northbourne (Middlesex, UK: Perennial Books, 1977), 7-8.

2. Seyyed Hossein Nasr, *Islamic Art and Spirituality* (Albany: State University of New York Press, 1987), 7–8.

3. John O'Donohue, *Beauty: The Invisible Embrace* (New York: HarperCollins, 2004), 3–4.

4. Ibid., 7.

5. Rumi, *The Essential Rumi*, translated by Coleman Barks with John Moyne et al. (Edison, NJ: Castle Books, 1997), 36.

Chapter 18: The Garden

1. Henry Corbin, *Creative Imagination in the Sufism of Ibn 'Arabi*, translated by Ralph Manheim (Princeton, NJ: Princeton University Press, 1981), 91.

2. Henry Corbin, *Spiritual Body and Celestial Earth: From Mazdean Iran to Shi'ite Iran*, translated by Nancy Pearson (Princeton, NJ: Princeton University Press, 1977), 224–25.

3. Hazrat Inayat Khan, *A Meditation Theme for Each Day: A Centenary Commemoration of the Birth of Hazrat Inayat Khan* (New Lebanon, NY: Omega Publications, 1982), 20.

4. Elizabeth Murray, *Cultivating Sacred Space: Gardening for the Soul* (San Francisco: Pomegranate, 1997), 126.

5. Ibid., 126–27.

Chapter 19: The Green Man

1. William Anderson, *The Green Man: The Archetype of Our Oneness with the Earth* (London and San Francisco: Harper Collins,

1990), 14.

2. John Fowles, *The Tree* (New York: The Ecco Press, 1983), 51.

3. Sara Sviri, *The Taste of Hidden Things: Images on the Sufi Path* (Inverness, CA: The Golden Sufi Center, 1997), 83.

Chapter 20: The Mirror and Transparency

1. Nasr, *Man and Nature,* 96-97.

2. Jacob Needleman, *What Is God?* (New York: Jeremy P. Tarcher/Penguin, 2009), 217.

Chapter 21: The Heart

1. Corbin, *Creative Imagination*, 221.

2. William Chittick, *The Sufi Path of Love: The Spiritual Teachings of Rumi* (Albany: State University of New York Press, 1983), 37.

3. Rumi, from "Two Kinds of Intelligence" in *This Longing: Poetry, Teaching Stories, and Selected Letters*, versions by Coleman Barks and John Moyne (Putney, VT: Threshold Books, 1988), 36.

4. Hazrat Inayat Khan, *The Complete Sayings of Hazrat Inayat Khan* (New Lebanon, NY: Sufi Order Publications, 1978), 24.

5. Edwin Bernbaum, *The Way to Shambhala: A Search for the Mythical Kingdom Beyond the Himalayas* (Los Angeles: Jeremy P. Tarcher, Inc. 1980), 144.

6. Ibid., 145.

7. Ibid.

8. Joseph Chilton Pearce, *Evolution's End: Claiming the Potential of Our Intelligence* (New York: HarperCollins, 1992), 105.

9. Ibid., 210.

10. Pearce, *The Death of Religion*, 130.

11. Doc Childre and Howard Martin with Donna Beech, *The HeartMath Solution* (New York: HarperSanFrancisco, 1999), 10.

12. Corbin, *Creative Imagination*, 230.

13. James Winston Morris, *The Reflective Heart: Discovering Spiritual Intelligence in Ibn 'Arabi's Meccan Illuminations* (Louisville, KY: Fons Vitae, 2005), 128.

14. Stephen Harrod Buhner, *The Secret Teachings of Plants: The Intelligence of the Heart in the Direct Perception of Nature* (Rochester, VT: Bear & Co., 2004), 121.

15. Thomas Berry, *The Dream of the Earth*. (San Francisco: Sierra Club Books, 1990), 212.

16. Matthew Fox, "Some Thoughts on Thomas Berry's Contribution to the Western Spiritual Tradition" in *Thomas Berry, Dreamer of the Earth: The Spiritual Ecology of the Father of Environmentalism*, edited by Ervin Laszlo and Allan Combs (Rochester, VT: Inner Traditions International, 2011), 22.

Chapter 22: Bringing It All Together

1. Chet Raymo, *Natural Prayers* (St. Paul, MN: Ruminator Books, 1999), xiv.

2. Mary Oliver, "Messenger" in *Thirst* (Boston: Beacon Press, 2006), 1.

Suggested Readings

(Books are listed related to chapter content and so may appear multiple times.)

Foreword

Broomfield, John. *Other Ways of Knowing: Recharting Our Future with Ageless Wisdom.* Rochester, VT: Inner Traditions International, 1997.

Nasr, Seyyed Hossein. *Man and Nature: The Spiritual Crisis of Modern Man.* London: Unwin Hyman Limited, 1990.

Ross, Nancy Wilson. *Buddhism: A Way of Life and Thought.* New York: Random House, 1981.

Introduction

Baigent, Michael. *Racing Toward Armageddon: The Three Great Religions and the Plot to End the World.* New York: HarperCollins, 2009.

Fox, Matthew. *Original Blessing: A Primer in Creation Spirituality.* Santa Fe, NM: Bear & Co., 1983.

Gorman, Max. *Stairway to the Stars: Sufism, Gurdjieff and the Inner Tradition of Mankind.* London: Aeon, 2010.

Haisch, Bernard. *The Purpose-Guided Universe: Believing in Einstein, Darwin, and God.* Franklin Lakes, NJ: New Page Books, 2010.

Passmore, John. *Man's Responsibility for Nature: Ecological Patterns and Western Traditions.* New York: Charles Scribner's Sons, 1974.

Raymo, Chet. *When God Is Gone Everything Is Holy: The Making of a Religious Naturalist.* Notre Dame, IN: Sorin Books, 2008.

Sheldrake, Rupert. *The Rebirth of Nature: The Greening of Science and God.* New York: Bantam Books, 1991.

Whitehead, Alfred North. *Science and the Modern World.* New York: New American Library, 1948.

Wilson, Peter Lamborn, Christopher Bamford, and Kevin Townley. *Green Hermeticism: Alchemy and Ecology.* Great Barrington, MA: Lindisfarne Books, 2007.

Chapter 1: Other Ways of Knowing

Barks, Coleman, with John Moyne et al. *A Year with Rumi: Daily Readings.* New York: HarperCollins, 2006.

Broomfield, John. *Other Ways of Knowing: Recharting Our Future with Ageless Wisdom.* Rochester, VT: Inner Traditions International, 1997.

Diamond, John, MD. *Your Body Doesn't Lie: How to Increase Your Life Energy through Behavioral Kinesiology.* New York: Warner Books, 1980.

Duerr, Hans Peter. *Dreamtime: Concerning the Boundary between Wilderness and Civilization.* Translated by Felicitas Goodman. Oxford and New York: Basil Blackwell, 1985.

Harner, Michael. *The Way of the Shaman: A Guide to Power and Healing.* San Francisco: Harper & Row, 1980.

Karagulla, Shafica, MD. *Breakthrough to Creativity: Your Higher Sense Perception.* Marina del Rey, CA: DeVorss, 1967.

Lawlor, Robert. *Voices of the First Day: Awakening in the Aboriginal Dreamtime.* Rochester, VT: Inner Traditions International, 1991.

Linn, Denise. *The Secret Language of Signs: How to Interpret the Coincidences and Symbols in Your Life.* New York: Ballantine Books, 1996.

Morgan, Marlo. *Mutant Message Down Under.* New York: HarperCollins, 1991.

Moss, Robert. *Conscious Dreaming: A Spiritual Path for Everyday*

Life. New York: Three Rivers Press, 1996.
———. *Dreamgates: An Explorer's Guide to the Worlds of Soul, Imagination, and Life Beyond Death*. New York: Three Rivers Press, 1998.
Pearce, Joseph Chilton. *The Death of Religion and the Rebirth of Spirit: A Return to the Intelligence of the Heart*. Rochester, VT: Park Street Press, 2007.
Pennick, Nigel. *Sacred Geometry: Symbolism and Purpose in Religious Structures*. San Francisco: Harper & Row, 1982.
Ross, T. Edward, and Richard D. Wright. *The Divining Mind: A Guide to Dowsing and Self-Awareness*. Rochester, VT: Destiny Books, 1990.
Sheldrake, Rupert. *Dogs That Know When Their Owners Are Coming Home: And Other Unexplained Powers of Animals*. New York: Crown Publishers, 1999.
Vaughan, Frances E. *Awakening Intuition*. Garden City, NY: Anchor Books, 1979.
Vitebsky, Piers. *The Shaman*. Boston: Little, Brown & Co., 1995.
Wolff, Robert. *Original Wisdom: Stories of an Ancient Way of Knowing*. Rochester, VT: Inner Traditions International, 2001.
Wright, Patricia C., and Richard D. Wright. *The Divining Heart: Dowsing and Spiritual Unfoldment*. Rochester, VT: Destiny Books, 1994.

Chapter 2: Science, Geometry, Pattern and Proportion, Encoding, and More

Albarn, Keith, and Jenny Miall Smith, Stanford Steeele, and Dinah Walker. *The Language of Pattern: An Enquiry Inspired by Islamic Decoration*. New York/London: Harper & Row/Thames and Hudson, 1974.
Ardalan, Nader, and Laleh Bakhtiar. *The Sense of Unity: The Sufi Tradition in Persian Architecture*. Chicago and London: University of Chicago Press, 1973.
Bohm. David. *Thought as a System*. London/New York: Routledge, 1994.

Suggested Readings

———. *Wholeness and the Implicate Order.* London: Routledge & Kegan Paul, 1980.
Citro, Massimo, MD. *The Basic Code of the Universe: The Science of the Invisible in Physics, Medicine, and Spirituality.* Rochester, VT: Park Street Press, 2011.
Critchlow, Keith. *Islamic Patterns: An Analytical and Cosmological Approach.* New York: Schocken Books, 1976.
———. *Order in Space: A Design Source Book.* London: Thames and Hudson, 1969.
———. *Time Stands Still: New Light on Megalithic Science.* London: Gordon Fraser Gallery, 1979.
Doczi, György. *The Power of Limits: Proportional Harmonies in Nature, Art, and Architecture.* Boulder, CO: Shambhala, 1981.
Dossey, Larry, MD. *Meaning and Medicine: Lessons from a Doctor's Tales of Breakthrough and Healing.* New York: Bantam Books, 1992.
Douglas-Klotz, Neil. *The Hidden Gospel: Decoding the Spiritual Message of the Aramaic Jesus.* Wheaton, IL: Quest Books, 1999.
Gleick, James. *Chaos: Making a New Science.* New York: Viking Penguin, 1987.
Humphrey, Caroline, and Piers Vitebsky. *Sacred Architecture.* Boston: Little, Brown & Co., 1997.
Lawlor, Robert. *Sacred Geometry: Philisophy and Practice.* London/New York: Thames and Hudson/Crossroad, 1982.
Lifesmith Classic Fractals. Preface by Jeff Berkowitz. *Fractal Cosmos: The Art of Mathematical Design.* Oakland, CA: Dharma Enterprises/Amber Lotus, 1994.
Linn, Denise. *The Secret Language of Signs: How to Interpret the Coincidences and Symbols in Your Life.* New York: Ballantine Books, 1996.
Michell, John. *City of Revelation: A Book of Forgotten Wisdom on the Proportions and Symbolic Numbers of the Cosmic Temple.* New York: David McKay Co., 1972.
———. *The Dimensions of Paradise: The Proportions and Symbolic

Suggested Readings

Numbers of Ancient Cosmology. San Francisco: Harper & Row, 1988.
Michell, John, with Allan Brown. *How the World Is Made: The Story of Creation According to Sacred Geometry.* Rochester, VT: Inner Traditions International, 2009.
Pennick, Nigel. *Magical Alphabets: The Secrets and Significance of Ancient Scripts, Including Runes, Greek, Ogham and Hebrew and Alchemical Alphabets.* York Beach, ME: Samuel Weiser, 1990.
——. *Sacred Geometry: Symbolism and Purpose in Religious Structures.* San Francisco: Harper & Row, 1982.
Purce, Jill. *The Mystic Spiral: Journey of the Soul.* London: Thames and Hudson, 1974.
Shah, Idries. The Sufis. Garden City, NY: Anchor Books, 1971.
Sheldrake, Rupert. *Morphic Resonance: The Nature of Formative Causation.* Rochester, VT: Park Street Press, 2009.
Watson, Lyall. *Lifetide: The Biology of the Unconscious.* New York: Bantam, 1980.

Chapter 3: The Music of the Spheres

Berendt, Joachim-Ernst. *Nada Brahma: The World Is Sound; Music and the Landscape of Consciousness.* Translated by Helmut Bredigkeit. Rochester, VT: Destiny Books, 1987.
——. *The Third Ear: On Listening to the World.* Translated by Tim Nevill. New York: Henry Holt & Co., 1992.
Campbell, Don. *The Mozart Effect: Tapping the Power of Music to Heal the Body, Strengthen the Mind, and Unlock the Creative Spirit.* New York: HarperCollins, 2001.
Citro, Massimo, MD. *The Basic Code of the Universe: The Science of the Invisible in Physics, Medicine, and Spirituality.* Rochester, VT: Park Street Press, 2011.
Halpern, Steven. *Tuning the Human Instrument: Keeping Yourself in Sound Health.* Belmont, CA.: Spectrum Research Institute, 1978.

Suggested Readings

Halpern, Steven, with Louis Savary. *Sound Health: The Music and Sounds that Make Us Whole*. San Francisco: Harper & Row, Publishers, 1985.

Jenny, Hans. *Cymatics*. Basel: Basilius Press, 1966.

Retallack, Dorothy. *The Sound of Music and Plants*. Santa Monica, CA: DeVorss, 1973.

Tame, David. *The Secret Power of Music: The Transformation of Self and Society through Musical Energy*. Wellingborough, UK: Turnstone Press Limited, 1984.

Tompkins, Peter, and Christopher Bird. *Secrets of the Soil*. New York: Harper & Row, 1989.

Chapter 4: Light

Bohm, David. *Wholeness and the Implicate Order*. London: Routledge & Kegan Paul, 1980.

Citro, Massimo, MD. *The Basic Code of the Universe: The Science of the Invisible in Physics, Medicine, and Spirituality*. Rochester, VT: Park Street Press, 2011.

Corbin, Henry. *The Man of Light in Iranian Sufism*. Translated by Nancy Pearson. Boulder, CO: Shambhala, 1978.

Cousens, Gabriel, MD. *Spiritual Nutrition and the Rainbow Diet*. Boulder, CO: Cassandra Press, 1986.

Fox, Matthew, and Rupert Sheldrake. *The Physics of Angels: Exploring the Realm Where Science and Spirit Meet*. New York: Harper Collins, 1996.

Gerber, Richard, MD. *Vibrational Medicine for the 21st Century: The Complete Guide to Energy Healing and Spiritual Transformation*. New York: HarperCollins, 2000.

———. *Vibrational Medicine: New Choices for Healing Ourselves*. Santa Fe, NM: Bear & Company, 1988.

Liberman, Jacob. *Light: Medicine of the Future: How We Can Use It to Heal Ourselves NOW*. Santa Fe, NM: Bear & Co., 1991.

Ott, John N. *Health and Light: The Effects of Natural and Artificial Light on Man and Other Living Things*. New York: Pocket

Suggested Readings

Books, 1976.

———. *Light, Radiation, and You: How to Stay Healthy.* Greenwich, CT: Devin-Adair, 1990.

Ross, T. Edward, 2nd. *The Healing Mind: The Way of the Dowser.* Danville, VT: American Society of Dowsers, 2013.

Russell, Peter. *From Science to God: The Mystery of Consciousness and the Meaning of Light.* Las Vegas, NV: Elf Rock Productions, 2002.

Shaykh Tosun Bayrak al-Jerrahi al-Helveti. *Suhrawardi: The Shape of Light.* Louisville, KY: Fons Vitae, 1998.

Wilson, Peter Lamborn. *Angels.* London: Thames and Hudson, 1980.

———. *Angels: Messengers of the Gods.* London and New York: Thames and Hudson, 1994.

Chapter 5: Earth

Benyus, Janine M. *Biomimicry: Innovation Inspired by Nature.* New York: HarperCollins, 1997.

Dass, Ram, and Paul Gorman. *How Can I Help? Stories and Reflections on Service.* New York: Alfred A. Knopf, 1985.

Gore, Al. *Earth in the Balance: Ecology and the Human Spirit.* New York: Plume, 1993.

Lauck, Joanne Elizabeth. *The Voice of the Infinite in the Small: Revisioning the Insect-Human Connection.* Mill Spring, NC: Swan.Raven & Co., 1998.

Lovelock, J. E. *Gaia: A New Look at Life on Earth.* Oxford: Oxford University Press, 1979.

McDonough, William, and Michael Braungart. Excerpt from "The Extravagant Gesture: Nature, Design and the Transformation of Human Industry," in *Choices for Sustainable Living.* Portland, OR: Northwest Earth Institute, 2007.

Rockefeller, Steven C., and John C. Elder, eds. *Spirit and Nature: Why the Environment Is a Religious Issue.* Boston: Beacon Press, 1992.

Tompkins, Peter, and Christopher Bird. *Secrets of the Soil.* New York: Harper & Row, 1989.

Chapter 6: Earth Energies

Berry, Thomas. *The Great Work: Our Way into the Future.* New York: Bell Tower/Crown, 1999.

Bord, Janet, and Colin Bord. *Earth Rites: Fertility Practices in Pre-Industrial Britain.* London and New York: Granada Publishing, 1983.

Devereux, Paul. *Re-Visioning the Earth: A Guide to Opening the Healing Channels between Mind and Nature.* New York: Fireside, 1996.

Feild, Reshad. *Here to Heal.* Longmead, UK: Element Books, 1985.

Graves, Tom. *Needles of Stone.* London: Turnstone Books, 1978.

Ingerman, Sandra. *Medicine for the Earth: How to Transform Personal and Environmental Toxins.* New York: Three Rivers Press, 2000.

Kimmerer, Robin Wall. *Braiding Sweetgrass: Indigenous Wisdom, Scientific Knowledge, and the Teachings of Plants.* Minneapolis, MN: Milkweed Editions, 2013.

Lonegren, Sig. *Labyrinths: Ancient Myths and Modern Uses.* Glastonbury, UK: Gothic Image Publications, 1991.

———. *Spiritual Dowsing.* Glastonbury, UK: Gothic Image Publications, 1986.

Mathews, John, and Caitlin Matthews. *The Western Way: A Practical Guide to the Western Mystery Tradition.* 2 vols. London: Arkana, 1985 and 1986.

Michell, John. *The Earth Spirit: Its Ways, Shrines, and Mysteries.* New York: Avon Books, 1975.

———. *The New View Over Atlantis.* San Francisco: Harper & Row, 1983.

Molyneaux, Brian Leigh. *The Sacred Earth.* Boston: Little, Brown & Co., 1995.

Pennick, Nigel. *The Ancient Science of Geomancy: Man in Harmony*

Suggested Readings

with the Earth. London: Thames and Hudson, 1979.

———. *Earth Harmony: Siting and Protecting Your Home—A Practical and Spiritual Guide*. London: Century Hutchinson Ltd., 1987.

Ross, T. Edward, and Richard D. Wright. *The Divining Mind: A Guide to Dowsing and Self-Awareness*. Rochester, VT: Destiny Books, 1990.

Swan, James A. *Nature as Teacher and Healer: How to Reawaken Your Connection with Nature*. New York: Villard Books, 1992.

———, ed. *The Power of Place: Sacred Ground in Natural and Human Environments*. Wheaton, IL: Quest Books, 1991.

Thom, Alexander. *Megalithic Lunar Observatories*. Oxford: Oxford University Press, 1971.

———. *Megalithic Sites in Britain*. Oxford: Oxford University Press, 1967.

Underwood, Guy. *The Pattern of the Past*. London: Abacus, 1972.

Vaughan-Lee. Llewellyn, ed. *Spiritual Ecology: The Cry of the Earth*. Point Reyes, CA: The Golden Sufi Center, 2016.

Versluis, Arthur. *Sacred Earth: The Spiritual Landscape of Native America*. Rochester, VT: Inner Traditions International, 1992.

Walters, Derek. *Feng Shui: The Chinese Art of Designing a Harmonious Environment*. New York: Fireside, 1988.

Watkins, Alfred. *The Old Straight Track: Its Mounds, Beacons, Moats, and Mark Stones*. London: Abacus, 1974.

Wright, Patricia C., and Richard D. Wright. *The Divining Heart: Dowsing and Spiritual Unfoldment*. Rochester, VT: Destiny Books, 1994.

Chapter 7: Harmony with the Cosmos

Berry, Thomas. *The Great Work: Our Way into the Future*. New York: Bell Tower/Crown, 1999.

Crawford, E. A. *The Lunar Garden: Planting by the Moon Phases*. New York: Weidenfeld & Nicholson, 1989.

Hageneder, Fred. *The Spirit of Trees: Science, Symbiosis, and Inspiration*. New York: Continuum, 2001.

Suggested Readings

House, Adrien. *Francis of Assisi: A Revolutionary Life*. Mahwah, NJ: Hidden Spring/Paulist Press, 2001.

Ladinsky, Daniel, translator. *Love Poems from God: Twelve Sacred Voices from the East and West*. New York: Penguin Compass, 2002.

Nasr, Seyyed Hossein. *The Garden of Truth: The Vision and Promise of Sufism, Islam's Mystical Tradition*. New York: Harper Collins, 2007.

Stella Natura: Working with Cosmic Rhythm: Information and Practical Advice for Home Gardeners and Professional Growers. Calendar published by Growing Biodynamics LLC, PO Box 783, Kimberton, PA 19442.

Thun, Maria, and Matthias Thun. *The North American Maria Thun Biodynamic Calendar*. Edinburgh: Floris Books.

Tompkins, Peter, and Christopher Bird, *Secrets of the Soil*. New York: Harper & Row, 1989.

Chapter 8: The Mineral Kingdom and Mountains

Ashe, Geoffrey. *The Ancient Wisdom: A Quest for the Source of Mystic Knowledge*. London: Macmillan, 1977.

Bennett, John G. *The Masters of Wisdom*. Wellingborough, UK: Turnstone Books, 1980.

Bernbaum, Edwin. *The Way to Shambhala: A Search for the Mythical Kingdom Beyond the Himalayas*. Los Angeles: Jeremy P. Tarcher, Inc., 1980.

Buhner, Stephen Harrod. *The Secret Teachings of Plants: The Intelligence of the Heart in the Direct Perception of Nature*. Rochester, VT: Bear & Co., 2004.

Callahan, Philip S. *Nature's Silent Music: A Rucksack Naturalist's Ireland*. Kansas City, MO: Acres USA Publications, 1982.

Corbin, Henry. *Spiritual Body and Celestial Earth: From Mazdean Iran to Shi'ite Iran*. Translated by Nancy Pearson. Princeton, NJ: Princeton University Press, 1977.

Evans-Wentz, W. Y. *Cuchama and Sacred Mountains*. Edited by Frank Waters and Charles L. Adams. Athens: Ohio University

Suggested Readings

Press, 1981.
Gerber, Richard, MD. *Vibrational Medicine for the 21st Century: The Complete Guide to Energy Healing and Spiritual Transformation.* New York: HarperCollins, 2000.
Gold, Peter. *Navajo and Tibetan Sacred Wisdom: The Circle of the Spirit.* Rochester, VT: Inner Traditions International, 1994.
Hilton, James. *Lost Horizon.* New York: William Morrow, 1933.
Kharitidi, Olga, MD. *Entering the Circle: The Secrets of Ancient Siberian Wisdom Discovered by a Russian Psychiatrist.* New York: HarperCollins, 1996.
LePage, Victoria. *Shambhala: The Fascinating Truth Behind the Myth of Shangri-la.* Wheaton, IL: Quest Books, 1996.
Trungpa, Chögyam. *Shambhala: The Sacred Path of the Warrior.* Boston and London: Shambhala, 1984.

Chapter 9: The World of Plants

Aburrow, Yvonne. *The Enchanted Forest: The Magical Lore of Trees.* Freshfields, Berkshire, UK: Capall Bann Publishing, 1993.
Altman, Nathaniel. *Sacred Trees: Spirituality, Wisdom, and Well-Being.* San Francisco: Sierra Club Books, 1994.
Bach, Edward, MD, and F. J. Wheeler, MD. *The Bach Flower Remedies.* New Canaan, CT: Keats Publishing, Inc. 1977.
Blamires, Steve. *Celtic Tree Mysteries: Practical Druid Magic and Divination.* St. Paul, MN: Llewellyn Publications, 2003.
Buhner, Stephen Harrod. *The Lost Language of Plants: The Ecological Importance of Plant Medicines to Life on Earth.* White River Junction, VT: Chelsea Green, 2002.
Cook, Roger. *The Tree of Life: Image for the Cosmos.* New York: Avon Books/Thames and Hudson, 1974.
Corbin, Henry. *Creative Imagination in the Sufism of Ibn 'Arabi.* Translated by Ralph Manheim. Princeton, NJ: Princeton University Press, 1981.
Cowan, Eliot. *Plant Spirit Medicine.* Newberg, OR: Swan.Raven & Co., 1995.
The Findhorn Community. *The Findhorn Garden: Pioneering a*

Suggested Readings

New Vision of Humanity and Nature in Cooperation. Forres, Scotland: Findhorn Press, 1988.

Giono, Jean. *The Man Who Planted Trees.* Chelsea, VT: Chelsea Green Publishing Company, 1985.

Gladstar, Rosemary. *Rosemary Gladstar's Herbal Recipes for Vibrant Health: 175 Teas, Tonics, Oils, Salves, Tinctures, and Other Natural Remedies for the Entire Family.* North Adams, MA: Storey Books, 2008.

Gladstar, Rosemary, and Pamela Hirsch. *Planting the Future: Saving Our Medicinal Herbs.* Rochester, VT: Healing Arts Press, 2000.

Graves, Robert. *The White Goddess: A Historical Grammar of Poetic Myth.* New York: Vintage Books, 1958.

Gurudas. *Flower Essences and Vibrational Healing.* San Rafael, CA: Cassandra Press, 1989.

Hageneder, Fred. *The Meaning of Trees: Botany, History, Healing, Lore.* San Francisco: Chronicle Books, 2005.

———. *The Spirit of Trees: Science, Symbiosis, and Inspiration.* New York: Continuum International, 2001.

Heaney, Seamus. *Sweeney Astray: A Version from the Irish.* New York: Farrar Straus Giroux, 1983.

Hill, Julia Butterfly. *The Legacy of Luna: The Story of a Tree, a Woman, and the Struggle to Save the Redwoods.* New York: HarperCollins, 2000.

LaFleur, William R. "Sattva, Enlightenment for Plants and Trees in Buddhism." In *The Language of the Birds: Tales, Texts, and Poems of Interspecies Communication*, edited by David M. Guss. San Francisco: North Point Press, 1985.

Margulis, Lynn. "Living by Gaia." In *Talking on the Water: Conversations about Nature and Creativity*, by Jonathan White. San Francisco: Sierra Club Books, 1994.

Martin, Laura C. *The Folklore of Trees and Shrubs.* Old Saybrook, CT: The Globe Pequot Press, 1992.

Mercatante, Anthony S. *The Magic Garden: The Myth and Folklore of Flowers, Plants, Trees and Herbs.* New York: Harper & Row, 1976.

Suggested Readings

Montgomery, Pam. *Plant Spirit Healing: A Guide to Working with Plant Consciousness.* Rochester, VT: Bear & Co., 2008.

Murray, Liz, and Colin Murray. *The Celtic Tree Oracle: A System of Divination.* New York: St. Martin's Press, 1988.

Nasr, Seyyed Hossein. *Man and Nature: The Spiritual Crisis of Modern Man.* London: Unwin Hyman Limited, 1990.

O'Keefe, J. G. *Buile Suibhne Geilt.* Bilingual edition, Irish Texts Society, 1913.

Paterson, Jacqueline Memory. *Tree Wisdom: The Definitive Guidebook to the Myth, Folklore and Healing Power of Trees.* San Francisco: Thorsons, 1996.

Schwenk, Theodor. *Sensitive Chaos: The Creation of Flowing Forms in Water and Air.* Translated by Olive Whicher and Johanna Wrigley. New York: Schocken Books, 1978.

Schwenk, Theodor, and Wolfram Schwenk. *Water: The Element of Life.* Translated by Marjorie Spock. Hudson, NY: Anthroposophic Press, 1989.

Scoble, Gretchen, and Ann Field. *The Meaning of Flowers: Myth, Language and Lore.* San Francisco: Chronicle Books, 1998.

Stein, Diane. *Essential Psychic Healing: A Complete Guide to Healing Yourself, Healing Others, and Healing the Earth.* Freedom, CA: Crossing Press, 2006.

———. *Natural Healing for Dogs and Cats.* Freedom, CA: The Crossing Press, 1993.

Suzuki, David, with Amanda McConnell and Adrienne Mason. *The Sacred Balance: Rediscovering Our Place in Nature.* Vancouver: Greystone Books, 2007.

Tompkins, Peter, and Christopher Bird. *The Secret Life of Plants.* New York: Harper & Row, 1973.

Thompson, William Irwin. *Imaginary Landscape: Making Worlds of Myth and Science.* New York: St. Martin's, 1989.

Uyldert, Mellie. *The Psychic Garden: Plants and Their Esoteric Relationship with Man.* Translated by H. A. Smith. Wellingborough, UK: Thorsons Publishers Ltd., 1980.

Suggested Readings

Weed, Susun S. *Healing Wise*. Woodstock, NY: Ash Tree Publications, 1989.

Wilson, Edward O. *The Diversity of Life*. Cambridge, MA: Belknap Press/Harvard University Press, 2010.

Wohlleben, Peter. *The Hidden Life of Trees: What They Feel, How They Communicate*. Translated by Jane Billinghurst. Vancouver and Berkeley: Greystone Books, 2016.

Wright, Machaelle Small. *Behaving as If the God in All Life Mattered: A New Age Ecology*. Jeffersonton, VA: Perelandra, 1987.

Chapter 10: The World of Animals

Andrews, Ted. *Animal-Wise: The Spirit, Language and Signs of Nature*. Jackson, TN: Dragonhawk Publishing, 1999.

Boone, J. Allen. *Kinship with All Life*. New York: HarperCollins, 1976.

Boulet, Susan Seddon, in Michael Babcock's *Susan Seddon Boulet: A Retrospective*. San Francisco: Pomegranate, 2000.

Cooper, J. C. *Symbolic and Mythological Animals*. London: Aquarian Press/HarperCollins, 1992.

Ford, Brian J. *The Secret Language of Life: How Animals and Plants Feel and Communicate*. New York: Fromm International, 2000.

Guss, David M. *The Language of the Birds: Tales, Texts and Poems of Interspecies Communication*. San Francisco: North Point, 1985.

Kinkade, Amelia. *The Language of Miracles: A Celebrated Psychic Teaches You to Talk to Animals*. Novato, CA: New World Library, 2006.

Masson, Jeffrey Moussaieff. *The Pig Who Sang to the Moon: The Emotional World of Farm Animals*. New York: Ballantine Books, 2003.

Pearce, Joseph Chilton. *Magical Child Matures*. New York: E. P. Dutton, 1985.

Randour, Mary Lou. *Animal Grace: Entering a Spiritual Relationship with Our Fellow Creatures*. Novato, CA: New World Library, 2000.

Sams, Jamie. *Earth Medicine: Ancestors' Ways of Harmony for Many Moons.* New York: HarperCollins, 1994.

Saunders, Nicholas J. *Animal Spirits.* Boston: Little, Brown & Co., 1995.

Shah, Idries. *The Sufis.* Garden City, NY: Anchor Books, 1971.

Shepard, Paul. *The Others: How Animals Made Us Human.* Washington, DC, and Covelo, CA: Island Press/Shearwater Books, 1996.

———. *Thinking Animals: Animals and the Development of Human Intelligence.* New York: Viking Press, 1978.

Shepard, Paul, and Barry Sanders. *The Sacred Paw: The Bear in Nature, Myth, and Literature.* New York: Viking Penguin, 1985.

Smith, Penelope. *Animal Talk: Interspecies Telepathic Communication.* Point Reyes Station, CA: Pegasus Publications, 1989.

———. *Animals: Our Return to Wholeness.* Point Reyes, CA: Pegasus Publications, 1993. (*Animals: Our Return to Wholeness* was later called *When Animals Speak.*)

———. *Animals in Spirit: Our Faithful Companions' Transition to the Afterlife.* New York/Hillsboro, OR: Simon & Schuster/Beyond Words, 2008.

———. *When Animals Speak: Advanced Interspecies Communication.* Hillsboro, OR: Beyond Words, 1999.

Waddell, Helen, translator. *Beasts and Saints.* Grand Rapids, MI: William B. Erdman, 1996.

Wootton, Anthony. *Animal Folklore, Myth and Legend.* Poole, Dorset, UK: Blandford Press, 1986.

Wright, Patricia C., and Richard D. Wright. *The Divining Heart: Dowsing and Spiritual Unfoldment.* Rochester, VT: Destiny Books, 1994.

Chapter 11: Air

DeBlieu, Jan. *Wind: How the Flow of Air Has Shaped Life, Myth, and the Land.* Boston/New York: Houghton Mifflin, 1999.

Fremedon, Ellen. *Windforest: Spirit Brooding on Brooding Spirit.* New York: Continuum, 2000.

Suggested Readings

Gold, Peter. *Navajo and Tibetan Sacred Wisdom: The Circle of the Spirit.* Rochester, VT: Inner Traditions International, 1994.

Khalsa, Dharma Singh, MD, and Cameron Stauth. *Meditation in Medicine: Activate the Power of Your Natural Healing Force.* New York: Pocket Books, 2001.

Watson, Lyall. *Heaven's Breath: A Natural History of the Wind.* New York: William Morrow & Co., 1984.

Chapter 12: The World of Birds

Aburrow, Yvonne. *Auguries and Omens: The Magical Lore of Birds.* Freshfields, Berkshire, UK: Capall Bann Publishing, 1994.

Ackerman, Diane. *Dawn Light.* New York: W. W. Norton & Co., 2009.

Armstrong, Edward A. *The Folklore of Birds.: An Enquiry into the Origins and Distribution of Some Magico-Religious Tranditions.* Boston: Houghton Mifflin, 1959.

Attar, Farid ud-Din. *The Conference of the Birds.* Translated by C. S. Nott. Boston: Shambhala, 1993.

Ford, Brian. *The Secret Language of Life: How Animals and Plants Feel and Communicate.* New York: Fromm International, 2000.

Gallico, Paul. *The Snow Goose.* New York: Alfred A. Knopf, 1941.

Matthiessen, Peter. *The Birds of Heaven: Travels with Cranes.* New York: North Point Press, 2001.

Nozedar, Adele. *The Secret Language of Birds: A Treasury of Myths, Folklore, and Inspirational True Stories.* London: Harper Element, 2006.

Winged Migration. This film is available in both DVD and VHS format. There is also a book explaining how the film was made by Jacques Perrin with text by Jean-Francois Mongibeaux. Translated by David Wharry. *Winged Migration*, France and San Francisco: Editions de Seuil/Chronicle Books, 2003.

Chapter 13: The World of Insects

Boone, J. Allen. *Kinship with All Life.* New York: Harper Collins, 1976.

Suggested Readings

Lauck, Joanne Elizabeth. *The Voice of the Infinite in the Small: Revisioning the Insect-Human Connection.* Mill Spring, NC: Swan.Raven & Co., 1998.

Mein, Annemieke. *The Art of Annemieke Mein: Wildlife Artist in Textiles.* Tunbridge Wells, UK/Woodstock, NY: Search Press Ltd./Arthur Schwartz & Co., 1994.

Morgan, Marlo. *Mutant Message Down Under.* New York: HarperCollins, 1991.

Northwest Earth Institute. *Choices for Sustainable Living.* Portland, OR: Northwest Earth Institute, 2007.

Ford, Brian. *The Secret Language of Life: How Animals and Plants Feel and Communicate.* New York: Fromm International, 2000.

Chapter 14: Water

Alexandersson, Olof. *Living Water: Viktor Schauberger and the Secrets of Natural Energy.* Translated by Kit and Charles Zweigbergk. Wellingborough, UK: Turnstone Press Ltd., 1982.

Bartholomew, Alick. *Hidden Nature: The Startling Insights of Viktor Schauberger.* Kempton, IL: Adventures Unlimited Press, 2005.

———. *The Spiritual Life of Water: Its Power and Purpose.* Rochester, VT: Park Street Press, 2010.

Batmanghelidj, F., MD. *Your Body's Many Cries for Water: You Are Not Sick, You Are Thirsty! Don't Treat Thirst with Medications.* Falls Church, VA: Global Health Solutions, 1995.

Citro, Massimo, MD. *The Basic Code of the Universe: The Science of the Invisible in Physics, Medicine, and Spirituality.* Rochester, VT: Park Street Press, 2011.

Coats, Callum. *Living Energies: An Exposition of Concepts Related to the Theories of Viktor Schauberger.* Bath, UK: Gateway Books, 1996.

Dossey, Larry, MD. *Space, Time and Medicine.* Boulder, CO: Shambhala, 1982.

Emoto, Masaru. *The Hidden Messages in Water.* Translated by

Suggested Readings

David A. Thayne. Hillsboro, OR: Beyond Words Publishing, 2004.

Flanagan, Patrick, and Gael Crystal Flanagan. *Elixir of the Ageless: You Are What You Drink.* Flagstaff, AZ: Vortex Press, 1986.

Rumi. *We Are Three: New Rumi Poems.* Translations by Coleman Barks. Athens, GA: Maypop Books, 1987.

Schwenk, Theodor. *Sensitive Chaos: The Creation of Flowing Forms in Water and Air.* Translated by Olive Whicher and Johanna Wrigley. New York: Schocken Books, 1978.

Schwenk, Theodor, and Wolfram Schwenk. *Water: The Element of Life.* Translated by Marjorie Spock. Hudson, NY: Anthroposophic Press, 1989.

Tompkins, Peter, and Christopher Bird. *Secrets of the Soil.* New York: Harper & Row, 1989.

Wright, Patricia C., and Richard D. Wright. *The Divining Heart: Dowsing and Spiritual Unfoldment.* Rochester, VT: Destiny Books, 1994.

Chapter 15: The World of Fish and Other Water Creatures

Corzine, Amy. *The Secret Life of the Universe: The Quest for the Soul of Science.* London: Watkins Publishing, 2008.

Ford, Brian J. *The Secret Language of Life: How Animals and Plants Feel and Communicate.* New York: Fromm International, 2000.

Kurlansky, Mark. *Cod: A Biography of the Fish That Changed the World.* New York: Penguin Books, 1998.

Montgomery, Sy. *The Soul of an Octopus: A Surprising Exploration into the Wonder of Consciousness.* New York: Atria Books/Simon & Schuster, 2015.

Nollman, Jim. *The Charged Border: Where Whales and Humans Meet.* New York: Henry Holt & Co., 1999.

———. *Spiritual Ecology: A Guide to Reconnecting with Nature.* New York: Bantam Books, 1990.

Remen, Rachel Naomi, MD. *My Grandfather's Blessings: Stories*

Suggested Readings

of Strength, Refuge, and Belonging. New York: Riverhead Books, 2000.

Shepard, Paul. *Nature and Madness.* San Francisco: Sierra Club Books, 1982.

Chapter 16: Art

Barks, Coleman. *The Essential Rumi: Versions by Coleman Barks.* New York: HarperCollins, 1995.

Boericke, Art, and Barry Shapiro. *Handmade Houses: A Guide to the Wood Butcher's Art.* San Francisco: Scrimshaw Press, 1973.

Burckhardt, Titus. *Sacred Art in East and West: Its Principles and Methods.* Translated by Lord Northbourne. Middlesex, UK: Perennial Books, 1977.

Charpentier, Louis. *The Mysteries of Chartres Cathedral.* Translated by Ronald Fraser. New York: Avon, 1975.

Coomeraswamy, Ananda K. *Christian and Oriental Philosophy of Art.* New York: Dover Publications, Inc., 1956.

Forel, Oscar. *Hidden Art in Nature: Synchromies.* New York: Harper & Row, 1972.

Goldsworthy, Andrew. *Andy Goldsworthy: A Collaboration with Nature.* New York: Harry N. Abrams, 1990.

———. *Stone.* New York: Harry N. Abrams, 1994.

Gluckman, Dale Carolyn. *Kimono as Art: The Landscapes of Itchiku Kubota.* San Diego, CA: San Diego Museum of Art/ Thames and Hudson, 2008.

Howard, Constance. *Inspiration for Embroidery.* Newton Centre, MA: Charles T. Branford Co., 1967.

Lindquist, Mark. *Sculpting Wood: Contemporary Tools and Techniques.* Worcester, MA: Davis Publications, Inc., 1986.

Mack, Daniel. *Making Rustic Furniture: The Tradition, Spirit, and Technique with Dozens of Project Ideas.* Asheville, NC: Lark Books, 1992.

Mathison, Vicki. *Dog Works: The Meaning and Magic of Canine*

Suggested Readings

Construction. Berkeley, CA: Ten Speed Press, 2000.
Mein, Annemieke. *The Art of Annemieke Mein: Wildlife Artist in Textiles.* Tunbridge Wells, UK/Woodstock, NY: Search Press Ltd./Arthur Schwartz & Co., 1994.
Miyawaki, Ayako. *Ayako Miyawaki: The Art of Japanese Applique.* Washington, DC: National Museum of Women in the Arts/Asahi Shimbun, 1991.
Nasr, Seyyed Hossein. *Islamic Art and Spirituality.* Albany, NY: State University of New York Press, 1987.
The Natural Home. London: Co and Bear Productions/DuMont monte UK, 2000.
O'Donohue, John. *Beauty: The Invisible Embrace.* New York: HarperCollins, 2004.
Ostergard, Derek E. *George Nakashima: Full-Circle.* New York: Weidenfeld and Neilson/American Craft Museum of American Craft Council, 1989.
Shapiro, Mark, ed. *A Chosen Path: The Ceramic Art of Karen Karnes.* Chapel Hill, NC: University of North Carolina Press, 2010.
Simon, Ellen. T*he Critter Book.* *New York:* Holiday House, 1940.
Warren, Verina. *Landscape in Embroidery.* London: B. T. Batsford, Ltd., 1986.

Chapter 17: Children and Nature

Carson, Rachel. *The Sense of Wonder.* New York: Harper & Row, 1965.
Cornell, Joseph Bharat. *Sharing the Joy of Nature: Nature Activities for All Ages.* Nevada City, CA: Dawn Publications, 1989.
———. *Sharing Nature with Children: A Parents' and Teachers' Nature-Awareness Guidebook.* Nevada City, CA: Ananda Publications, 1979.
Fuhrman, Joel, MD. *Eat for Life: The Breakthrough Nutrient-Rich Program for Longevity, Disease Reversal, and Sustained Weight Loss.* New York: HarperCollins, 2020.
Louv, Richard. *Last Child in the Woods: Saving Our Children from*

Suggested Readings

Nature-Deficit Disorder. Chapel Hill, NC: Algonquin Books, 2006.

Pearce, Joseph Chilton. *The Death of Religion and the Rebirth of Spirit: A Return to the Intelligence of the Heart.* Rochester, VT: Park Street Press, 2007.

———. *Evolution's End: Claiming the Potential of Our Intelligence.* New York: HarperSanFrancisco, 1992.

———. *Magical Child Matures.* New York: E. P. Dutton, Inc., 1985.

Robbins, John. *The Food Revolution: How Your Diet Can Help Save Your Life and Our World.* San Francisco: Conari Press, 2010.

Chapter 18: The Garden

Berrall, Julia. *The Garden: An Illustrated History.* New York: Viking Press, 1966.

Bremness, Lesley. *The Complete Book of Herbs.* New York: Viking Penguin, 1994.

Coleman, Eliot. *The New Organic Grower's Four-Season Harvest: How to Harvest Fresh Organic Vegetables from Your Home Garden All Year Long.* Post Mills, VT: Chelsea Green, 1992.

———. *The Winter Harvest Handbook: Year Round Vegetable Production Using Deep Organic Techniques and Unheated Greenhouses.* White River Junction, VT: Chelsea Green Publishing, 2009.

Corbin, Henry. *Creative Imagination in the Sufism of Ibn 'Arabi.* Translated by Ralph Manheim. Princeton, NJ: Princeton University Press, 1981.

———. *Spiritual Body and Celestial Earth: From Mazdean Iran to Shi'ite Iran.* Translated by Nancy Pearson. Princeton, NJ: Princeton University Press, 1977.

Creasy, Rosalind. *Edible Landscaping: Now You Can Have Your Gorgeous Garden and Eat It Too!* San Francisco: Sierra Club Books, 2010.

Dawson, Adele G. *Herbs, Partners in Life: Healing, Gardening, and Cooking with Wild Plants*. Rochester, VT: Healing Arts Press, 2000.

Dervish, H. B. M. *Journeys with a Sufi Master*. London: Octagon Press, 1987.

Garland, Sarah. *The Herb Garden*. New York: Viking Penguin, 1984.

Gustafson, Herb. *The Art of Japanese Gardens*. New York: Sterling Publishing Co., 1999.

———. *Making Bonsai Landscapes*. New York: Sterling Publishing Co., 1999.

Hemenway, Toby. *Gaia's Garden: A Guide to Home-Scale Permaculture*. White River Junction, VT: Chelsea Green, 2001.

Hill, Lewis. *Successful Cold-Climate Gardening*. Brattleboro, VT: Stephen Greene Press, 1981.

Hill, Lewis, and Nancy Hill. *The Flower Gardener's Bible: Time-Tested Techniques, Creative Designs, and Perfect Plants for Colorful Gardens.*. North Adams, MA: Storey Books, 2003.

Hobhouse, Penelope. *Penelope Hobhouse's Gardening through the Ages: An Illustrated History of Plants and Their Influences on Garden Style—from Ancient Egypt to the Present Day*. New York: Simon & Schuster, 1992.

Jay, Roni. *Gardens of the Spirit: Create Your Own Sacred Spaces*. New York: Sterling Publishing Co., 1998.

———. *Sacred Flowers: Creating a Heavenly Garden*. Hillsboro, OR: Beyond Words Publishing, 1997.

Khan, Hazrat Inayat. *A Nature Theme for Each Day: A Centenary Commemoration of the Birth of Hazrat Inayat Khan*. New Lebanon, NY: Omega Press, 1982.

Landsberg, Sylvia. *The Medieval Garden*. New York: Thames and Hudson, 1996.

Larkcom, Joy. *The Salad Garden*. New York: The Viking Press, 1984.

McIntyre, Anne. *Flower Power: Flower Remedies for Healing Body and Soul through Herbalism, Homeopathy, Aromatherapy, and Flower Essences*. New York: Henry Holt & Co., 1996.

Mercatante, Anthony S. *The Magic Garden: The Myth and Folklore*

Suggested Readings

of Flowers, Plants, Trees and Herbs. New York: Harper & Row, 1976.
Murray, Elizabeth. *Cultivating Sacred Space: Gardening for the Soul.* San Francisco: Pomegranate, 1997.
Patnaik, Naveen. *The Garden of Life: An Introduction to the Healing Plants of India.* New York: Doubleday, 1993.
Paul, Anthony, and Yvonne Rees. *The Water Garden.* New York: Penguin Books, 1986.
Powell, Claire. *The Meaning of Flowers: A Garland of Plant Lore and Symbolism from Popular Custom and Literature.* Boulder, CO: Shambhala, 1979.
Schenk, George, *Moss Gardening: Including Lichens, Liverworts, and Other Minatures.* Portland, OR: Timber Press, 1997.
Seward, Barbara. *The Symbolic Rose.* New York: Columbia University Press, 1960.
Seymour, John. *The Self-Sufficient Gardener: A Complete Guide to Growing and Preserving All Your Own Food.* Garden City, NY: Doubleday & Co./Dolphin Books, 1979.
Shepard, Paul. *Man in the Landscape: A Historic View of the Esthetics of Nature.* New York: Alfred A. Knopf, 1967.
Slawson, David A. *Secret Teachings in the Art of Japanese Gardens.* Tokyo and New York: Kodansha International Ltd., 1987.
Titley, Norah, and Frances Wood. *Oriental Gardens.* London: British Library Board, 1991.
Tompkins, Peter, and Christopher Bird, *Secrets of the Soil.* New York: Herper & Row, 1989.
Wright, Machaelle Small. *Perelandra Workbook II: Co-Creative Energy Processes for Gardening, Agriculture and Life.* Jeffersonton, VA: Perelandra Ltd., 1990.
Wydra, Nancilee. *Feng Shui in the Garden: Simple Solutions for Creating Comforting, Life-Affirming Gardens of the Soul.* Lincolnwood, IL: Contemporary Books, 1997.

Chapter 19: The Green Man

Anderson, William. *The Green Man: The Archetype of Our Oneness with the Earth.* London and San Francisco: Harper Collins, 1990.

Suggested Readings

Fowles, John. *The Tree*. New York: Ecco Press, 1983.

Sviri, Sara. *The Taste of Hidden Things: Images on the Sufi Path*. Inverness, CA: Golden Sufi Center, 1997.

Chapter 20: Mirror and Transparency

Berman, Morris. *Coming to Our Senses: Body and Spirit in the Hidden History of the West*. New York: Bantam Books, 1990.

Nasr, Seyyed Hossein. *Man and Nature: The Spiritual Crisis of Modern Man*. London: Unwin Hyman Limited, 1990.

Needleman, Jacob. *What Is God?* New York: Jeremy P. Tarcher/Penguin, 2009.

Shepard, Paul. *Man in the Landscape: A Historic View of the Esthetics of Nature*. New York: Alfred A. Knopf, 1967.

Chapter 21: The Heart

Bernbaum, Edwin. *The Way to Shambhala: A Search for the Mythical Kingdom Beyond the Himalayas*. Los Angeles: Jeremy P. Tarcher, Inc., 1980.

Berry, Thomas. *The Dream of the Earth*. San Francisco: Sierra Club Books, 1990.

Bruchac, Joseph. *Entering Onondaga*. Austin, TX: Cold Mountain Press, 1978.

Buhner, Stephen Harrod. *The Secret Teachings of Plants: The Intelligence of the Heart in the Direct Perception of Nature*. Rochester, VT: Bear & Co., 2004.

Childre, Doc, and Howard Martin with Donna Beech. *The HeartMath Solution*. New York: HarperCollins, 1999.

Chittick, William. *The Sufi Path of Love: The Spiritual Teachings of Rumi*. Albany: State University of New York Press, 1983.

Citro, Massimo, MD. *The Basic Code of the Universe: The Science of the Invisible in Physics, Medicine, and Spirituality*. Rochester, VT: Park Street Press, 2011.

Corbin, Henry. *Creative Imagination in the Sufism of Ibn 'Arabi*. Translated by Ralph Manheim. Princeton, NJ: Princeton University Press, 1981.

Suggested Readings

———. *Spiritual Body and Celestial Earth: From Mazdean Iran to Shi'ite Iran*. Translated by Nancy Pearson. Princeton, NJ: Princeton University Press, 1977.

de Hartog, Jan. *The Centurion*. New York: Harper and Row, 1989.

Fox, Matthew. "Some Thoughts on Thomas Berry's Contributions to the Western Spiritual Tradition." In *Thomas Berry, Dreamer of the Earth: The Spiritual Ecology of the Father of Environmentalism*. Edited by Ervin Laszlo and Allan Combs. Rochester, VT: Inner Traditions, 2011.

Hartmann, Thom. *The Prophet's Way: Touching the Power of Life*. Northfield, VT: Mythical Books, 1997.

Khan, Hazrat Inayat. *The Complete Sayings of Hazrat Inayat Khan*. New Lebanon, NY: Sufi Order Publications, 1978.

Morris, James Winston. T*he Reflective Heart: Discovering Spiritual Intelligence in Ibn 'Arabi's Meccan Illuminations*. Louisville, KY: Fons Vitae, 2005.

Rumi. *This Longing: Poetry, Teaching Stories, and Selected Letters*. Versions by Coleman Barks and John Moyne. Putney, VT: Threshold Books, 1988.

Chapter 22: Bringing It All Together

Oliver, Mary. *Thirst*. Boston: Beacon Press, 2006.

Raymo, Chet. *Natural Prayers*. St. Paul, MN: Ruminator Books, 1999.

Postscript

AT VARIOUS times my husband and I offered a series of classes based on books that we felt could help people with their lives: *The Education of Little Tree* by Forrest Carter, *Mutant Message Down Under* by Marlo Morgan, *Ishmael* by Daniel Quinn, *The Last Barrier* by Reshad Feild, and *The Prophet's Way* and *Last Hours of Ancient Sunlight* by Thom Hartmann. The intent was to show similar attitudes of respect for nature coming through different traditions: Native American, Australian Aboriginal, the animal world, Sufi mysticism, and Judaeo/Christian service. *Last Hours* then painted a grim picture of our world situation but suggested positive actions that could begin to turn things around. One participant wrote that this was the most powerful reading and discussion series in which she had ever taken part. Through many traditions came one voice, one message.

I also highly recommend the novels of Jan de Hartog. Jan was a great storyteller, a sailor, a Quaker, and a dowser, and he wrote about moral dilemmas and how one finds one's way through them. There are no saccharine endings, but always there is the powerful feeling of Presence and that "infinite ocean of light and love."